"Lee Williams has provided a marvelous re[...] and couple therapists in training. Building c[...] structure, the 7 Cs, Williams orients the [...] essential aspects of couple assessment. Strongly anchored in evidence-based methods and in a broad integrative view of couple assessment, this book provides a comprehensive yet highly coherent way of understanding couple relationships. This book should be a part of every course in couple therapy and a part of every couple therapist's library."

— **Jay Lebow, PhD,** *ABPP, LMFT, Family Institute at Northwestern, Family Process Editor*

"Thorough assessment is a crucial part of effective therapy with couples. Lee Williams has done masterful work in providing a critically needed book on dyadic assessment. In this well-written and engaging book, Lee clearly describes the 7 Cs assessment approach, an evidence-informed and transtheoretical framework. Lee walks the novice clinician through each assessment component – assessment structure, content areas to explore, challenges with couples, and using assessment to inform interventions. This book is essential reading for all students in training as well as seasoned couple therapists."

— **Adrian Blow, PhD**, *Professor at Michigan State University*

ASSESSMENT IN COUPLE THERAPY

This innovative text offers a simple but comprehensive framework for couple assessment that integrates research and information on couples from a wide range of models.

Using the 7 Cs as a basis for guiding assessment, chapters move through key areas of couple functioning including communication, conflict resolution, culture, commitment, caring and sex, contract, and character. An additional chapter on children also offers insights into assessment of couples who parent. Offering a broad and accessible framework that can be applied to a variety of theoretical perspectives, the book highlights how the 7 Cs can be used to inform both assessment and treatment of couples. Numerous case examples are interwoven throughout the text to demonstrate how therapists may utilize this approach to work with a diverse client base.

Written in an accessible style, *Assessment in Couple Therapy* is an essential tool for students of marriage and family therapy and beginning therapists, as well as seasoned mental health professionals working with couples in a range of settings.

Lee Williams, PhD, is a professor of marital and family therapy at the University of San Diego, where he has taught since 1993. He is a licensed marriage and family therapist and clinical fellow at AAMFT (American Association of Marriage and Family Therapy).

ASSESSMENT IN COUPLE THERAPY

Navigating the 7 Cs of Relationships

Lee Williams, PhD

Routledge
Taylor & Francis Group

NEW YORK AND LONDON

Cover image: © Getty Images

First published 2022
by Routledge
605 Third Avenue, New York, NY 10158

and by Routledge
4 Park Square, Milton Park, Abingdon, Oxon, OX14 4RN

Routledge is an imprint of the Taylor & Francis Group, an informa business

© 2022 Lee Williams

Library of Congress Cataloging-in-Publication Data
Names: Williams, Lee, LMFT, author.
Title: Assessment in couple therapy : navigation the 7 C's of relationships / Lee Williams, PhD.
Description: New York, NY : Taylor & Francis, 2022. | Includes bibliographical references and index.
Identifiers: LCCN 2021032754 (print) | LCCN 2021032755 (ebook) | ISBN 9780367752996 (hardback) | ISBN 9780367753160 (paperback) | ISBN 9781003161967 (ebook)
Subjects: LCSH: Couples therapy. | Family psychotherapy. | Marital psychotherapy.
Classification: LCC RC488.5 .W5616 2022 (print) | LCC RC488.5 (ebook) | DDC 616.89/1562—dc23
LC record available at https://lccn.loc.gov/2021032754
LC ebook record available at https://lccn.loc.gov/2021032755

ISBN: 978-0-367-75299-6 (hbk)
ISBN: 978-0-367-75316-0 (pbk)
ISBN: 978-1-003-16196-7 (ebk)

DOI: 10.4324/9781003161967

Typeset in Bembo
by Apex CoVantage, LLC

CONTENTS

List of Tables   ix

Foreword   x

Acknowledgments   xiii

1 Introduction: Assessing Couples Using The 7 Cs   1

2 Getting Started – Structuring Assessment   7

3 Communication   25

4 Conflict Resolution   42

5 Culture   58

6 Commitment   75

7 Caring   86

8 Assessing a Couple's Sexual Relationship   99

9 Contract   120

10 Character   133

11 Children: An Eighth C?   153

12 Moving Beyond the Initial Assessment   160

    References   173
    Index   182

TABLES

3.1	Assessment of Communication Skills	40
4.1	Assessing How Couples Handle Conflict	56
5.1	Assessment Questions for Intercultural Couples	72
5.2	Assessment from a Sociocultural Perspective	74
6.1	An Inventory of Commitment	84
7.1	Assessing Caring Behaviors	98
8.1	General Assessment Questions for Sex	117
9.1	Assessment of Contract Issues	131
10.1	Assessing Character Features	151
11.1	Assessment Questions Regarding Children	158
12.1	Example of Feedback Using the 7 Cs	165

FOREWORD

First, let us note that the history of empirically based couple assessments and therapies has generally covered a period from about 1970 to date (2021). I will not quote specific references in this foreword noting that many of the sources are cited in the book itself. Over this period the overall divorce rate has hovered between 40–50% of married couples. Notably, the divorce rate among formerly married partners is even greater, as is the case for couples dealing with partners' individual problems in areas of emotionality, behavioral problems, or health concerns.

Thus, investigators of couple assessments and therapies have experienced 40-plus years of developing couple assessment, couple intake and interview procedures, as well as couple (and individual) treatments. There have been several books written about treating difficult couples with relationship problems combined with individual partners' problems and when to separate the treatment of individual problems from treating, or not treating them, within a couple therapy format. Significant gains have been made in offering alternative couple treatment models and developing empirically based assessment instruments, assessment procedures, and manualized treatment approaches.

The assessment model forming the basis of couple assessment in this book is called the 7 Cs. I first developed this model in the 1990s with my graduate students at the VA Hospital in San Diego in association with the

School of Medicine, University of California San Diego Department of Psychiatry. At the time, I was a licensed clinical psychologist and Director of the VA Family Mental Health Program and Professor of Psychiatry (my entire career).

We wanted to have an operational behavioral systems framework for assessing couples that beginning therapists could understand and use successfully to complete a multi-faceted five-session assessment of distressed couples and also provide feedback and treatment planning understandable to the couples. In 1994, 1999, and 2003 the 7 Cs model was elaborated on in relevant journals and books. As you will learn, the 7 Cs includes interviews and observations of the following couple relationship attributes: Character, Cultural and Ethnic factors, Contract, Commitment, Caring, Communication, and Conflict Resolution.

In 2001 I had the opportunity to engage in some outside teaching at the nearby University of San Diego Marital and Family Therapy Program. While there I also had the fortunate opportunity to meet Professor Lee Williams. While I was teaching classes at USD, Lee asked if he could engage in some clinical work by treating couples at the VA. I held a weekly Friday morning supervision seminar that he attended from 2001–2005 when I retired. Lee continued attending seminars until 2020. This was a great opportunity for the VA patients, Lee, and me to gain clinical experience and, importantly, to provide supervision as a cotherapist with dozens of trainees learning couple and family therapy over 20 years. Accordingly, Lee had experiential access to applying, teaching, and indeed further developing the 7 Cs model over two decades.

There are a number of special purposes and features of this book. First, this book amounts to a 20-year update and upgrade of the 7 Cs Model of Couple Assessment. A detailed chapter on assessing a couple's sexual relationship (a critical part of Caring within a relationship) is added as a very important activity to assess for virtually all couples. There is also an eighth C proposed for many couples – a detailed chapter on assessing potential conflicts and strengths related to raising children, both parenting a couple's own children and dealing with stepchildren, as well as coparenting children from former relationships.

Second, the book is dedicated to clinical skills associated with couple assessment and multi-method assessments using paper and pencil instruments.

Third, the book is written in fine detail to help advance the clinician's assessment skills and related interventions from the first minute of the couple's intake meeting, through the proposed five sessions of assessment, up to the last minute of providing feedback to the couple and treatment planning, if appropriate.

Finally, the book also serves as a complete training manual for not only couple therapy trainees, but it can also be easily adopted by supervisors of trainees no matter their theoretical approach to understanding distressed couples.

To summarize, this book is written primarily for clinical trainees learning to assess couples no matter their educational discipline. It works for family therapy trainees, Masters and PhD level psychologists in training, social work students, nurse practitioners, and interested medical school students or psychiatry residents in training. The book can also be applied by accomplished therapists as a new tool and model of assessment for distressed couples. The book is so detailed that it can be a great resource for supervisors of all persuasions. The book describes what needs to be learned about the couple to determine relationship and individual partner function and dysfunction using the expanded 7 Cs, what specific questions and observations to employ throughout the five-session assessment process, and how to prepare feedback and a treatment plan for each couple being assessed.

This is a book that won't be left sitting on your shelf. It will be reviewed for important and necessary conduct in sessions before and after the couple meetings by trainees and their supervisors. Enjoy learning.

Gary R. Birchler, PhD

ACKNOWLEDGMENTS

I would like to first acknowledge Dr. Gary Birchler for introducing me to the 7 Cs. I have found the 7 Cs extremely valuable in my clinical work as a couple therapist. I would like to also thank the following students who helped with the preparation of the manuscript: Mckenna Ebiner, Helene Glatter-Goetz, and Jordan Harber.

1

INTRODUCTION

Assessing Couples Using The 7 Cs

Do you remember your experience of learning how to drive a car? You had to learn the rules of the road before you were given a permit to get behind the wheel. You then had to develop several new skills for operating the vehicle, including learning how to properly accelerate a car, how to stop it, and how to park. Once you had mastered these basic skills on a driving course or quiet street, you then ventured out into the real world where you encountered more complex situations. Now you were on the road with other drivers, sometimes in heavy traffic. Or you were learning to drive at much higher speeds on a highway or interstate, which sometimes required merging onto a lane with fast moving traffic. Not only did you have to pay attention to what you were doing, but you also had to be aware of what other drivers on the road were doing. Some have said that learning to drive is one of the most complex activities that we regularly engage in.

If the divorce rate in our society is any indicator, then building a successful marriage or committed intimate relationship is an equally if

DOI: 10.4324/9781003161967-1

not more challenging endeavor than driving. Human beings are psychologically complex, which can make a relationship between two of them all the more complicated. In fact, some have questioned why it is easier to get a marriage license than a driver's license. As a couple therapist, you will have to confront this complexity when working with couples. Fortunately, couple therapists and marital researchers have accumulated a wealth of knowledge on what it takes to build a successful relationship. This book was written to help you access some of the best ideas in the field to guide your work with couples.

To organize all of these concepts or ideas into a coherent picture, you will be learning the 7 Cs framework (Birchler et al., 1999). Gary Birchler, who was director of the couple clinic at the San Diego Veteran's Administration Hospital, was the originator of the 7 Cs. As a training site, Gary taught all the therapists to use the 7 Cs during their internship. I learned of the 7 Cs when I began to volunteer as a therapist with Gary at the VA. I was immediately drawn to the framework due to its simplicity, as well as its ability to integrate ideas from a number of different sources into a coherent framework. It soon became my mental file cabinet for organizing the wealth of information I was accumulating from various models I learned, from research, and from my own clinical experience.

If you are new to working with couples, you may be asking yourself some of the following questions:

"Where do I start in my assessment?"

"What is important to focus on when assessing couples?"

"How do I know I am doing a thorough assessment and that I am not missing anything important?"

"How do I translate what I am learning about the couple through assessment into an effective treatment plan?"

"How will I know if the treatment I chose is working?"

This book will attempt to answer these and other questions for you.

I have made the decision to focus this book primarily on assessment for two reasons. First, it became apparent in reading the literature that there are no contemporary books that focus on couple assessment. Current books on assessment in the family therapy field combine family and couple assessment. In fact, I am co-author of one of these books, *Essential Assessment Skills for Couples and Family Therapists* (Williams et al.,

2011). Unfortunately, books like this only devote a chapter or two on how to do an assessment that focuses specifically on couples. Because assessing couple functioning is very different from assessing individual or family functioning, it would be helpful to have a book that provides a more comprehensive description on how to do couple assessment.

Although an older book on couple assessment exists (Karpel, 1994), it makes no reference to current evidence-based approaches like emotionally focused therapy or integrative behavioral couple therapy. Furthermore, John Gottman's research, which has profoundly shaped our understanding of intimate relationships in marriage, is not addressed either. Therefore, this book fulfills a need for a contemporary guide on how to assess couples that reflects our current understanding of couples and how to treat them.

Second, this book focuses on assessment because it is the key to effectively treating couples. Without a proper understanding of a couple and their dynamics, your treatment interventions are likely to be misguided or ineffective (J. S. Gottman & J. M. Gottman, 2015). Think of assessment as the foundation for treatment. You can't build a 3,000 square foot house on a foundation that can only support a 1,500 square foot house. Much like the foundation of a house, assessment dictates what can and can't be done in treatment. If you don't include certain areas of a couple's functioning into your assessment, then you won't know if these areas need attention or repair. This book will help you feel more confident that you have an adequate understanding of a couple upon which to build your treatment.

Before describing the 7 Cs framework in more detail and how to use the book, I would like to make explicit some of the philosophies that have informed how the book was written. First, although the book primarily focuses on assessment, it was also written with treatment in mind. Assessment and treatment are closely linked, like two sides of the same coin. Despite its focus on assessment, the book is written in such a way that implications for treatment will be clearly evident.

Second, the book emphasizes a strength-based approach to assessment. As you go through the book, you will be encouraged to examine not only areas where the couple may be struggling, but also areas where the couple is doing well or has strengths. For example, some chapters include a discussion of protective factors that can be assessed. These strengths should be celebrated and built upon.

Third, the book emphasizes an integrative perspective rather than promoting one particular model over another. Offering an integrative perspective is not unique to this book. However, what makes the 7 Cs unique as an integrative framework is its simplicity. In the couple therapy course that I teach, beginning therapists like how easy the framework is to grasp and how quickly it orients them on what to look for in a couple's functioning. At the same time, more experienced clinicians will appreciate the elegance and flexibility of the framework to integrate and organize a wealth of information for working with couples. You will find that the 7 Cs framework can expand and grow to accommodate the new knowledge you will accumulate as you gain more experience working with couples.

Fourth, the book primarily focuses on how evidence-based approaches and research can inform our understanding of couples. In their book *10 Principles for Doing Effective Couples Therapy*, Julie Gottman and John Gottman (2015) state that the first principle is to use research-based methods to treat couples. Consistent with this recommendation, the concepts described in this book have been drawn primarily from the leading couple therapy models with strong research support for their effectiveness. This includes models like emotionally focused therapy (EFT), the Gottman approach to couple therapy, integrative behavioral couple therapy (IBCT), and the Prevention and Relationship Enhancement Program (PREP). Although the emphasis in this book is on concepts from empirically supported models, you can also integrate ideas from other family systems models (e.g., narrative, Bowen, structural) using the framework. The 7 Cs framework allows one to assemble the best ideas that each of these models has to offer in understanding couples, much like a compilation of the best hits from various artists. In addition, insights from research or your own clinical experience can be integrated into the 7 Cs.

Each C within the framework has at least one chapter devoted to it (one of the Cs has two chapters). The first C is **communication**. Communication is not only the basis for intimacy, but it also helps couples handle the inevitable problems that arise in any intimate relationship. Good communication skills help couples discuss these issues in an effective manner, thereby reducing the likelihood that conflict will escalate as couples try to address their issues. This chapter will help you evaluate a couple's ability to effectively communicate in terms of discussing issues and building intimacy.

Couples will also benefit from having effective **conflict resolution skills** when addressing issues, the focus of the next C. This chapter will help you assess a couple's ability to handle conflict in relationships, including learning how to identify problematic interactional cycles that create dissatisfaction in relationships.

The third C is devoted to examining **culture**. Culture is broadly defined to include not just race or ethnicity, but also religion, sexual orientation, socioeconomic background, and nationality, among other factors. The chapter will look at how culture can impact couples in a variety of ways. The chapter will first explore how cultural differences between partners can impact relationships, as well as how intercultural couples attempt to manage these differences. The second section will discuss the need to assess sociocultural factors for all couples to determine the role that larger social systems have upon couples, including the potential to influence power dynamics within relationships. Cultural factors can also play a role in the level of acceptance that couples experience, which is addressed in the last section. For example, intercultural couples or same-sex couples may experience a lack of acceptance from family, friends, or others, which can impact social support and create minority stress.

Commitment, the fourth C, is essential to sustaining a relationship through difficult times. This chapter will focus on assessing a couple's level of commitment, as well as various factors that can impact their level of commitment. This assessment will also inform how you might nurture or strengthen commitment in a couple's relationship.

Love is the cornerstone of intimate relationships. The expression of love through **caring** behaviors will be the next C. This chapter will emphasize the importance of assessing the couple's love languages for expressing love. It will also consider other aspects of caring, such as offering emotional support and nurturing a strong connection in the relationship.

Sex is another important element of caring that can enhance a couple's relationship. Due to its importance and complexity, a separate chapter is devoted to assessing a couple's sexual relationship. This chapter will review important principles to guide assessment, common causes of sexual problems, and specific considerations for various sexual disorders. A section is also devoted to assessing issues related to pornography use, which is an increasingly common concern.

All relationships carry expectations between partners. These expectations form the basis of a couple's **contract**, the sixth C. This chapter will explore how to assess four common contract issues that occur in relationships. This will include assessing the extent to which a couple has been able to repair their relationship after a serious violation of the contract (e.g., infidelity) by working through important tasks (the 6 As).

Individual attributes can impact relationships in both positive and negative ways. For example, each person's personality can influence the relationship, including creating the potential for conflict. Similarly, mental illness and physical illness can also impact a couple's relationship. Therefore, this chapter will focus on the seventh C, exploring how individual attributes or **character** are important to assess in relationships.

The 7 Cs above apply across all couples. However, for couples with **children**, I recommend that this be considered as a possible eighth C due to the significant role of parenting in a couple's relationship. Therefore, this chapter will explore potential relationship challenges couples face while parenting. It will also include unique challenges that couples may face if they bring children from previous relationships into their current one.

The book will conclude with how to take the information learned from each of the Cs to organize feedback for a couple and develop a treatment plan. It will also describe how you can use the 7 Cs framework to integrate interventions from various treatment models if you so desire.

Although separate chapters are devoted to each of the Cs, you will quickly notice that the various Cs are connected. For example, cultural factors can shape a number of the other Cs, including how couples communicate or the expectations they have for each other (contract). Likewise, a couple's effectiveness in communicating may impact their ability to resolve issues in the other Cs. Therefore, it can be helpful to be aware of the possible interconnections between the Cs during your assessment.

Before delving into each of the Cs, the next chapter discusses how therapists might structure their assessment to collect information for each of the Cs. This chapter begins by describing a five-session model for conducting a couple assessment. This is followed by a discussion of various assessment techniques that can be used to collect information during an assessment.

2

GETTING STARTED –
STRUCTURING ASSESSMENT

Holly and Ross, both 38, are sitting in your office for their initial therapy session. You know from the intake phone call that they have been married for 10 years, and that they have two sons ages 6 and 4. The couple complains of "communication problems" and are seeking your help to improve their marriage. Where do you begin?

This chapter will explore how to begin couple therapy so you can successfully help a couple like Holly and Ross. The first section will describe a structure or blueprint you can follow when conducting a couple assessment. The second section will briefly review tools or techniques you can use in assessment to collect information.

Structure of the Initial Sessions

Starting couple therapy off properly is important to the success of therapy. The following five-session model can help you accomplish many of the important tasks that need to happen during assessment to create the

DOI: 10.4324/9781003161967-2

proper foundation for treatment. This model can be adapted as necessary based on the couple's needs or the therapist's preferences.

Session One – Initial Interview

Several important tasks need to happen in the first session (Patterson et al., 2018; Williams et al., 2011). One of the most important tasks is to properly join with the couple. Otherwise, the couple may not come back for a second session. Building a strong relationship with the couple will also build trust, which will encourage the couple to be more open in disclosing sensitive information during assessment.

Therapists can face several challenges when joining with couples. Sometimes couples want you to play referee and tell them whose perspective is right. However, taking one partner's side will likely damage your relationship with the other partner. A better approach is to find something to validate within both partners' perspectives.

Another potential challenge you may face when joining with couples is that one partner dominates the conversation. In these situations, it is important to draw out the quieter partner. Sometimes this may require politely blocking the dominant partner from speaking to create space for the other partner to speak. During the assessment, it is important to set the expectation that you want to get both partners' perspectives.

Joining with a couple can also be more difficult if you feel more aligned with one partner versus the other. Obviously, it is important to remain balanced in joining with both partners. Sometimes you may feel more aligned with one client if they appear to present better than the other individual. For example, it may be easier to feel more aligned with the withdrawn partner rather than the angry and critical partner. Recognizing the underlying hurt that fuels the anger and criticism can help you feel more compassion for this individual and provide a more balanced perspective. In some cases, it may be easier for you to see or understand one partner's perspective because you share similar backgrounds, experiences, or values. These situations have the potential to create a bias, especially if it taps into a personal issue for the therapist. For example, you may be more sympathetic to an overfunctioner's complaints about their underfunctioning mate if you experienced a similar issue in a current or past relationship. The first step is to be aware that this is occurring, which will aid you in keeping your bias in check. However, it may also be important to seek out supervision or consultation to make sure your bias is not coming out in ways that are not evident to you.

Providing informed consent is another key task in the initial session. You will need to cover a number of topics with your couple, including confidentiality and its limits, fees, your credentials (e.g., disclosure if you are unlicensed), and when therapy might be terminated. Questions that come up during the informed consent process might give you clues about the couple. For example, if a couple asks whether the courts can have access to therapy records when discussing confidentiality, this might be an indicator that the couple is preparing for divorce and a possible custody battle.

Establishing goals for therapy is also an important task in the initial interview. You can typically ask the couple directly what their goals are for therapy or how they hope therapy will be helpful. It is important to ask both partners for their goals, and not to assume that the couple shares the same perspective on what the problems are or how therapy can help. As you listen to them describe their goals and the problems in the relationship, you will need to evaluate if the couple is appropriate for conjoint therapy. For example, severe intimate partner violence would be a contraindication to doing conjoint work.

The initial interview is also when assessment of the couple begins. A lot of assessment information can be collected while determining goals for therapy. As the couple describes their issues or goals, you will be able to develop some hypotheses about the couple. In addition, below are some questions that you may want to ask or consider during initial assessment to learn more about the couple:

When did the problems first begin?

What changes were happening in the couple's life when the problems began?

Why is the couple seeking therapy now?

What has the couple attempted to do to solve or cope with the problems?

Has the couple had previous therapy? If so, what was helpful and what was not helpful?

Is one person seen as having the problem, or is it viewed as a couple issue?

What are the couple's thoughts or hypotheses about why the problems exist?

Who initiated therapy? How did the partner respond to the request to do therapy?

What does the couple see as the strengths of each other and their relationship?

The final task in the initial interview is to build a sense of hope. Many couples may be discouraged due to the length of time they have been distressed. Buongiorno and Notarius (1992, as cited in Gottman, 1999, p. 235) found that couples wait on average 6 years before seeking out help. You can build a sense of hope in several ways, such as pointing out the couple's strengths or factors that could lead to a positive outcome in therapy. For example, you might note the couple's strong commitment to one another, or the couple's willingness to look at their own actions rather than blaming their partner, both positive indicators of success in therapy. If time permits, you could also consider beginning the relationship history (see session 2). Memories of the beginning of the relationship are typically positive and remind the couple why they fell in love with each other.

If you are going to ask your couple to complete assessment instruments, then the best time to do this is before, during, or after the initial session. As will be discussed shortly, assessment instruments can provide a lot of helpful information. One strategy is to have clients complete the inventories during the initial visit. If possible, it is best if clients can complete the instruments immediately before or after the session so that it does not detract from session time. An alternative strategy is to mail the instruments in advance or give them to the couple at the end of the initial session to complete at home and return at the next visit. Compliance in completing and returning the assessment instruments is somewhat lower if the couple completes them at home, although most clients will make the effort to complete and return them. Regardless of the approach that is used, couples should be instructed to complete the instruments independently of one another.

Session Two – Communication Sample and Relationship History

In the second session, you will meet with the couple conjointly to do a communication sample and relationship history. It often works best to do the communication sample first given that it is time limited. The communication sample provides you an opportunity to observe how the couple communicates while trying to solve a problem. When setting the exercise up, ask the couple to identify a problem of moderate intensity (around a 5 on a 1- to 10-point scale in terms of difficulty), and then instruct them to try to solve the problem for 10 minutes while you observe. For some couples, you may need to initially redirect them to talk to each other since you are strictly taking an observing role. After about 10 minutes, you can debrief the exercise with the couple, such as asking them if this is representative of what happens at home. The majority of couples will report that the exchange is very similar to what happens at home, although perhaps with less intensity. If a couple reports that the exchange was more productive than usual, then you can explore from a solution-focused perspective what was different so you can build upon this exception.

The majority of the second session is devoted to doing a relationship history. However, it is up to your discretion as to how much time you want to devote to the relationship history. I was originally trained to conduct detailed relationship histories using the Structured Initial Interview (Hiebert et al., 1993), which could last three to five sessions depending upon the length of the couple's relationship. In contrast, integrative behavioral couple therapy (Christensen et al., 2015) only devotes a small part of the initial interview to the relationship history, with primary focus on understanding what attracted both partners to one another.

Obviously, the amount of time that you devote to doing a relationship history will determine the amount of information and level of detail you obtain. If time is limited, it is often most beneficial to focus primarily on the couple's courtship. The courtship offers important information about what attracted the couple to each other (character), how they developed their bond (caring), and why they decided to spend their future together (commitment). The "seeds of divorce" are also often evident in the courtship (conflict resolution) for many couples. For example, a couple's first major fight often exposes the fault lines in a relationship that later lead the couple to break up. The courtship is also a critical time in the relationship where couples must navigate any cultural differences and establish a workable contract, as well as establish communication patterns. Finally, the positive memories associated with their courtship can create a sense of hope and optimism in the room, as well as remind the couple why they invested in the relationship in the first place.

When doing a relationship history, it is often best to proceed in a somewhat chronological order, beginning with inquiring how the couple first met. Good follow up questions include, "What was your first impression of your partner when you met?" and "What attracted you to your partner?" You might also ask if they found anything strange about their partner. These questions can illuminate important character features, including each person's strengths. It can also be helpful to ask if their initial impressions of the partner changed over time. For example, did they form a more favorable impression as they got to know the partner better (especially if the initial impressions were not favorable), or did a concern about the partner's character emerge?

In terms of caring, it can be important to explore what activities the couple did during their courtship to build their bond, and to inquire if any changes occurred during the course of the relationship (e.g., when children arrived). It can also be helpful to ask questions like, "How did you know that your partner loved you?" or "How did you show your partner that you cared for them?" Also, asking who initiated the first date and took the initiative to plan future dates or activities may provide clues as to who the pursuer is in the relationship.

Sex is another vital area to explore in the couple's relationship history. For example, it is helpful to know when the couple became sexually active in their relationship, and what this meant in terms of the relationship. For some couples, becoming sexually active can be a sign of increased commitment to the relationship. You can also ask if the couple has been satisfied with the frequency and quality of their sexual relationship, and if there have been any significant changes during the relationship in terms of frequency or quality. Related questions might be, "Has there been any conflict about sex in the relationship?" and "Who typically initiates sexual activity?"

When exploring the couple's relationship history, it is recommended that you explore important decisions made by the couple. For example, how did the couple decide to set up their finances? Did they have separate or joint accounts, and why? These decisions sometimes reflect how couples think about autonomy in the context of the relationship. How did they make other important decisions in their life, such as buying their first home, starting a family, or relocating for a new opportunity? Has the way the couple makes decisions changed over time? Conflict over important decisions could point to possible contract issues. It is also important to evaluate if one person has had significantly more influence over decision-making, suggesting a possible power differential in the relationship.

When exploring the couple's courtship, a number of questions may yield important insight about the couple's commitment, as well as potentially remind the couple why they fell in love with each other. For example, how and when did the couple choose to date each other exclusively? When and why did they choose to live together? Was this done out of convenience, or did the couple view this decision as a step toward increased commitment? At what point did each begin to think of marriage or the other as a possible mate for life? Were there any unplanned pregnancies prior to marriage, and how did this influence the couple's decision to get married or remain together? You can also ask if they have ever questioned their partner's commitment to the relationship, and if so, why. For example, did the couple experience any infidelities? Have they ever perceived their partner as being over-involved in work, hobbies, friends, or their families of origin?

It is also important to explore if the couple has any significant cultural differences (race/ethnicity, nationality, religion, etc.), and how these differences have impacted their relationship. In addition, how did the couple navigate these differences in the beginning of the relationship? How do they navigate these differences now?

It can also be helpful to explore how family and friends responded to the couple's relationship. What did family and friends think of the relationship? What were the concerns if they had any? For example, did they have concerns about the mate's character (e.g., abusive, mental health, personality) or was it tied to cultural concerns (not approving of the partner's race, ethnicity, religion, etc.)? How does the couple currently relate to each partner's extended family? Do they get along well with both extended families or have there been issues? What role do cultural factors have in how a couple relates to their respective families of origin?

It is also important to explore what conflict has looked like in the couple's relationship. For example, a good question to ask is, "When did you have your first major fight and what was it about?" The first fight often exposes a perpetual problem in the couple's relationship, which if not properly managed, can eventually lead to further conflict and even termination of the relationship. It can also be helpful to ask if the couple has experienced much conflict during the relationship, and if there have been periods of more or less conflict. In addition, you can ask, "What issues do you generally have conflict over?" These issues will sometimes point to unresolved contract issues. In addition, you should inquire how the couple handles conflict, and if there have been any changes over time in how they handle conflict. The answers may provide important clues regarding the couple's communication skills and ability to manage conflict, including possible negative interactional patterns or vicious cycles.

Throughout the history, you also want to inquire about major life transitions and events, including the impact they had upon the relationship. For example, you might ask the couple how their relationship changed after they began living together, or after they got married. For many couples, having children is a major transition. Therefore, you may want to ask questions like, "How did your relationship change after the arrival of children?" and "Were there any major disagreements about parenting?"

You should also explore if other major life events have occurred for the couple (e.g., death in the family, retirement, major health or mental health issues, unemployment) and how the couple navigated these events. In addition to looking at their impact, it can be helpful to ask how the couple was able to cope with the stress associated with these events to uncover the couple's strengths and resiliency.

This list is not exhaustive of the questions that you might ask during a relationship history. When conducting a relationship history, it is important to be curious as to why events unfolded in the manner in which they did rather than simply be a recorder of events on a timeline. For example, an unplanned pregnancy will ideally make you curious as to how this happened. Did they use some type of method of pregnancy prevention that failed, or was the couple not taking steps to prevent an unwanted pregnancy? One couple admitted that they had not been using any birth control measures. When this was explored further, the therapist discovered the couple had never discussed using birth control measures, which was an indicator of their conflict avoidance pattern. So, your curiosity about why events happened and how the couple responded to the events may lead you to probe further by asking additional questions. You are encouraged to design or tailor your questions to each couple's history.

As you learn about the various Cs throughout the rest of the book, this will also prompt you to ask additional questions to fill in your knowledge of each C. For example, you may learn that the couple had to navigate one partner having a major health crisis. Knowing that offering emotional support is an important component of caring will likely prompt you to ask how they supported each other through this difficult time, and if they experienced any challenges in this area.

Sessions Three and Four – Individual Sessions

In this assessment model, the third and fourth sessions are devoted to learning more about each partner's individual history, which can offer important contextual information about how each person interacts in the relationship. For example, Vanessa complained that Tyrese was emotionally unavailable to her. Tyrese admitted that this was indeed the case, and he attributed this to a "wall" that he put up to protect himself. In the individual history, Tyrese described a childhood of neglect and abuse from his mother and sister. He also admitted that two prior wives had been unfaithful. As a result of these experiences, Tyrese said it was very difficult for him to trust others. The individual history provided the therapist helpful information on the origins of the wall.

Before you do an individual session with each partner, you will need to decide in advance what information, if any, will be kept confidential. Some therapists follow a no secrets policy, which essentially means that they can share any information learned in the individual sessions with the partner in a conjoint session if it is deemed helpful or necessary to the couple's work in therapy. In contrast, other therapists promise to keep any information learned in the individual sessions confidential if the client requests it. There are pros and cons to each approach. If you keep material learned in individual interviews confidential, then clients may share information they want kept secret from their partner, but it is critical information to know because it informs therapy in a significant way. For example, individuals might share that they are having an affair, which would make therapy contraindicated for many therapists. However, confidentiality would prevent you from sharing why conjoint therapy is no longer feasible. With the no secrets policy, you are not going to keep a secret that could potentially damage your relationship with the other partner. However, critical information such as an individual's affair may be withheld if the couple knows the therapist practices a no secrets policy, so the therapist may be unaware that this is why therapy is unsuccessful. Regardless of the approach used, you need to be explicit with the couple in advance on your policy regarding confidentiality when doing individual sessions.

When doing the individual histories, you will want to explore a number of areas. One area that is often helpful to assess is the family of origin. When exploring the family of origin, it is important to be aware of any past neglect or abuse, which can leave a legacy in terms of future intimate relationships much like it did for Tyrese. It can also be helpful to explore what was modeled in terms of intimate relationships in the family of origin. For example, Mark felt that his mother dominated his father. Mark believed that his father was a weak man, and he was determined to be the opposite of his father. However, in an attempt to be different from his father, Mark went to the opposite extreme of being unwilling to be influenced by his mate. In this model, only a portion of the individual session is devoted to looking at the family of origin, which is often sufficient in identifying some key themes. However, some therapists (particularly those who favor a transgenerational perspective) may want to expand the assessment model by devoting more time to exploring the family of origin, perhaps by doing a detailed genogram (McGoldrick et al., 2020) for each partner.

Briefly exploring the individual's academic and occupational history can also yield some important clues in some cases. One man described how he was always getting into trouble as a child in elementary school. When asked why, the man replied that he was constantly being reprimanded for getting out of his seat. This was an important clue to discovering that the man had undiagnosed ADHD upon further assessment. Be sure to ask about any military service as part of your assessment, especially given some veterans can suffer from PTSD or other issues (e.g., traumatic brain injuries) that can impact relationships.

Another important area to inquire about are previous romantic relationships because you may discover that individuals replicate patterns across relationships. For example, Yolanda would often overfunction in her relationships. She would eventually get to the point where she would be exhausted and fed up with overfunctioning in the relationship, and she would eventually decide to leave her partner. However, she would then enter into another relationship where she would once again fall into the overfunctioning role. Seeing this repetitive pattern helped Yolanda recognize that she could not place all the blame on her current partner for the problems in the relationship, and that she would need to examine why she was always in the overfunctioning role.

As part of your assessment, you should inquire if there is any history of mental illness and substance abuse. This should include whether the individual had any previous suicide attempts, as well as the circumstances around these attempts. This can help you determine if the individual may be at current risk of hurting themselves. If the individual has a current mental health diagnosis, you will need to evaluate if the individual is being properly treated and the impact on the couple's relationship (see Chapter 10 on character). Likewise, you will need to determine if current substance use is creating problems for either an individual or the relationship, and whether a referral for treatment needs to be made.

In addition to exploring individual histories, the individual interviews should be used to assess for safety concerns, especially intimate partner violence (IPV). Individuals may be reluctant to disclose violence in the relationship in a conjoint session, especially if they fear their partner's reprisal. Depending upon the nature and severity of the violence, conjoint therapy might be contraindicated. Chapter 4 on conflict resolution includes a section on assessing intimate partner violence and the factors that may indicate whether conjoint therapy is feasible or not. If an individual discloses violence and fears retribution, then you may need to make an exception to a no secrets policy if the disclosure puts the individual at significant risk for violence (Bograd & Mederos, 1999).

Session Five – Feedback Session

The fifth session is devoted to giving the couple feedback. In the feedback session, you will be telling the couple what you learned about them, including both their strengths and areas of growth. Chapter 12 will discuss how the 7 Cs can be an effective tool for organizing feedback for a couple. You will also be outlining for the couple how you envision therapy will help them. The couple should be able to see a connection between the feedback you provide them about their relationship and the treatment plan.

In many cases, you may need to do one or more additional assessment sessions before you are ready to do a feedback session. This happens all the time, so don't feel pressured to give your feedback in the fifth session if you are not ready. At the same time, you don't want to extend assessment too long to be sure everything is crystal clear before giving any feedback. Your understanding of the couple will evolve as you provide feedback and begin to intervene. If you have a clear understanding of the couple's cycle and two or three points within each of the Cs, then you are probably ready to provide feedback to the couple.

Some therapists are concerned that couples will be impatient with a formal assessment approach that takes four or more sessions. Fortunately, most couples understand the need for a therapist to learn about the couple's relationship in order to offer an informed perspective on how to treat the issues. If clients express concerns about the length of the assessment process, it is important to emphasize that therapy will be more effective and efficient if you are working from a clear understanding of the relationship. In much the same way that we expect doctors to run some tests before recommending major surgery, therapists need to do a good assessment to understand what the best treatment will be.

It is also possible that therapists might wonder about the need to do a formal assessment. As noted previously, a good assessment will help the therapist make good choices in terms of how to proceed with treatment. If a good assessment is not done, then problems in the treatment phase are more likely to emerge. For example, therapists may make a less than ideal choice in terms of the treatment approach, or they get stuck in therapy because they are missing a crucial piece of information. The assessment phase also lets therapists develop a strong therapeutic alliance, which may be helpful when the therapist begins to challenge clients to change. Finally, therapists need to appreciate that assessment can be a form of intervention. When one therapist asked how the couple was doing before starting another assessment session, they responded that they were doing significantly better. Surprised, the therapist asked why the couple was doing so much better. The couple reported that after the therapist mapped out their cycle in the last session, they decided that they needed to find a way to break the cycle, which they were able to figure out on their own.

Tools for Assessment

You have a number of tools at your disposal when you are conducting a couple assessment. The remainder of the chapter will focus on describing three primary tools that therapists use during assessment: clinical questions, observation, and assessment instruments.

Clinical Questions

Asking clients questions is the primary assessment tool that therapists rely upon in assessment. Clinical questions are excellent at accessing what clients are thinking or feeling. They are also well suited for learning how clients behave, especially regarding behaviors that are done in private. However, one of the potential limitations of asking clients questions is that they may answer them in such a way as to make themselves look good, which is referred to as social desirability. Therefore, we always need to be mindful that a client's need to be viewed in a positive light may influence how accurately they answer our questions. For example, individuals may underreport the amount of alcohol they consume to avoid judgment about their drinking. Creating safety in the therapeutic relationship is one of the best measures the therapist can take to help minimize social desirability.

A client's ability to answer our questions is also dependent upon their level of insight. Some clients will have difficulty describing what they think, feel, or do when asked. Some clients, for example, do not value examining their emotional experience, and therefore may have difficulty answering how they feel or finding the words to express their emotions.

Finally, we rely on our clients to be cooperative in answering questions. Fortunately, this is more often a problem for clients mandated or forced to come to therapy, and it is less of a concern for couples who typically are voluntarily seeking help.

When asking questions, it is important to consider whether you want to ask a closed-ended or open-ended question (Williams et al., 2011). For close-ended questions, the answer to the question is offered or implied.

For example, a therapist might ask, "Are you satisfied with the frequency in which you have sex?" The implied answer is either yes or no, or to express some level of satisfaction (e.g., "I am very satisfied"). Closed-ended questions limit or define what type of answers are being sought.

In contrast, open-ended questions do not offer or suggest what the answers should be, giving individuals a lot of latitude on how to interpret and answer a question. An example of an open-ended question is, "How is sexual intimacy in your relationship?" A client could respond to this question in several ways, such as stating how often they have sex, their satisfaction with the quality of sex, or something entirely different (e.g., sexual preferences).

Open-ended questions are often good introductory questions for exploring a new topic. They make fewer assumptions about what the answer should be and are helpful in understanding what is most salient from the client's perspective. Closed-ended questions can be helpful if the therapist wants to obtain some specific information. For example, after learning that the client is concerned about the frequency of sex in the relationship through an open-ended question, the therapist might follow up by asking a closed-ended question to learn how satisfied the client is with the couple's sexual encounters when they do happen.

When asking closed-ended questions, the therapist should carefully consider what answer choices are offered. In some cases, asking a client using a scaling question will provide a more nuanced answer than asking a question that can be answered with a simple yes or no. For example, a client may be asked to rate on a scale from 1 to 10 how satisfied they are in their sexual relationship versus simply being asked if they are satisfied with it. It is also important that the answers that are offered are exhaustive of the possibilities. For example, it will be problematic if the therapist asks a male client if they are heterosexual or gay, excluding the possibility that the client might identify as bisexual.

Observation

Another important assessment tool that therapists rely upon is clinical observation (Balderrama-Durbin et al., 2020; Williams et al., 2011). As Yogi Berra once said, "You can observe a lot by just watching."

For example, the communication sample described earlier allows the therapist to directly observe how the couple communicates and solves problems. However, most observation does not happen during formal interventions like the communication sample. Rather, it happens as the therapist watches how the couple responds to each other throughout the session.

Observations can enhance your understanding of the couple in a variety of ways. For example, you may be able to directly observe the couple's negative interactional cycle in session. If you observe that one partner remains silent when the other partner is critical, then you might hypothesize that the couple engages in a demand-withdraw cycle. It is also helpful to observe how well individuals manage their emotions during sessions. Do they remain consistently calm, or does one or both become easily dysregulated? For couples who become more easily emotionally dysregulated, treatment may need to address this directly as an issue (e.g., time outs, emotional regulation skills). It is also important to assess for strengths through observation. For example, does the couple show any positive affect or behaviors (e.g., holding hands) toward each other? Is the couple able to be vulnerable with one another? Finally, observing the couple over time may provide important clues as to whether the couple is improving and their readiness for termination.

Assessment Instruments

Using assessment instruments in couple therapy can provide you with valuable information that can help you in developing your understanding of a couple (Balderrama-Durbin et al., 2020; Williams et al., 2011). Assessment instruments provide a quick and efficient means of collecting information about a couple. The information obtained from instruments may save you considerable time compared to asking all of these questions through clinical interviewing. Furthermore, some clients may be willing to disclose sensitive information such as intimate partner violence or sexual problems on an assessment instrument rather than volunteering this information in therapy. Assessment instruments also provide quantifiable data, which can be helpful in determining how a particular couple compares to other couples. For example, administering an instrument that measures marital quality can help you evaluate the couple's level of distress compared to other clinical or nonclinical couples.

Despite their advantages, it is also important to be mindful of their limitations. Assessment instruments rely on closed-ended, forced-choice responses. Although this is helpful in quantifying information, it also lacks the richness and nuances that qualitative data from clinical interviewing can provide. Used together, information from assessment instruments and clinical interviewing will ideally complement each other. Instruments also require time to score, although many brief instruments can be easily and quickly scored. Finally, although many instruments may be obtained for free, others may need to be purchased.

In light of the potential advantages and limitations, many therapists find it desirable to administer a small number of assessment instruments to couples. If you use assessment instruments, including a measure of relationship quality is recommended. One measure that clinicians frequently use is the Dyadic Adjustment Scale (Spanier, 1976), which is a 32-item measure of relationship adjustment. A shorter, 14-item version of the instrument also exists (Busby et al., 1995). Another potential measure to use is the Couple Satisfaction Index (Funk & Rogge, 2007), which focuses on satisfaction. The Couple Satisfaction Index is available in versions that contain 4, 16, or 32 items. Be aware that many other measures of relationship quality also exist. For example, the Marital Satisfaction Inventory-Revised (Snyder, 1997) is an instrument composed of 150 true-false questions. Although much longer, it offers a wealth of information on couples, including scores on 13 scales (e.g., communication, problem-solving, sex, financial disagreement). As you can see, instruments that measure relationship quality can vary in length. Therefore, you will need to weigh the potential information that longer instruments can provide with the additional time and effort it takes to complete and score these instruments, as well as potential costs.

Some therapists also like to include a measure of how likely the couple is to divorce. One commonly used measure to do this is the Marital Status Inventory (Weiss & Cerrato, 1980), which measures the steps that individuals have taken toward divorce. According to Whiting and Crane (2003), a score of 4 and above for husbands and a score of 5 and above for wives is an indicator of severe marital distress. Another alternative is the Marital Instability Index (Edwards et al., 1987).

It is strongly recommended that you include a measure to assess for intimate partner violence. Best practice recommends using more than one assessment technique for assessing intimate partner violence (Bradford, 2010). In addition to using assessment instruments, therapists should also inquire about intimate partner violence during the individual interview. The Conflict Tactics Scale (Straus, 1979) and the Revised Conflict Tactic Scale (Straus et al., 1996) are two examples of instruments that are used to screen for intimate partner violence. The Conflict Tactics Scale is a brief, 15-item measure of verbal aggression and physical violence, as well as reasoning (a constructive approach to conflict). The Revised Conflict Tactics Scale is significantly longer with 78 items but provides scores on six rather than three scales. These include physical assault, psychological aggression, negotiation, injury, sexual coercion, and a total score. In addition to these measures, other instruments are also available for screening for intimate partner violence.

Given how common depression is among individuals presenting for therapy, you may also want to include a measure that screens for depression. In fact, relationship distress can be a contributing factor to depression. There are a wide variety of instruments available, including instruments such as the PHQ-9 (Spitzer et al., 1999), the Beck Depression Inventory II (Beck et al., 1996), and the CES-D (Radloff, 1977), just to name a few.

Depending upon your approach or the population with which you work, you may want to include other measures in your assessment packet. For example, a therapist working with a military or veteran population may want to include a measure to screen for PTSD. You also have the ability to administer select instruments at a later time to couples based on their unique set of concerns. For example, you might have a couple take a personality instrument (see Chapter 10) if you sense that differences in personality may be playing a significant role in the relationship. Or you might administer an ADHD screening instrument to someone that you suspect might have undiagnosed ADHD.

Conclusion

This chapter has explored how to structure the initial sessions with a couple. The initial interview has several critical tasks associated with it, such as joining, providing informed consent, establishing goals, beginning assessment, and building hope. A communication sample and relationship history are conducted in the second assessment session. The next sessions are devoted to doing an individual history with each partner, followed by a session devoted to giving the couple feedback on their relationship and how therapy might help them.

3

COMMUNICATION

Being able to effectively communicate is important to intimate relationships as it allows individuals to share their thoughts and feelings with each other. This sharing ultimately becomes the basis for developing intimacy. Couples also need effective communication skills in order to discuss the inevitable problems that arise in any intimate relationship. Poor communication skills when facing these problems can increase conflict. This chapter will help you evaluate the couple's ability to effectively communicate with one another. Using insights from this assessment, you would be able to guide couples on how to improve their communication so they can better handle conflict and deepen their intimacy.

A Model for Understanding Communication

Imagine for a moment that a couple is in conversation. At any one moment, one person is the speaker, and the other person is the listener. In this speaker-listener exchange, there are four steps that occur in the

DOI: 10.4324/9781003161967-3

communication process. In the first step, the speaker must decide what message they would like to convey to the listener. In the second step, the speaker chooses how to express what they are thinking or feeling, either verbally or nonverbally (often both). The third step in the process is for the listener to receive the speaker's message. Receiving the message means the listener hears what the speaker is saying, as well as noticing any nonverbal cues (e.g., body language). In the final step, the listener must interpret the meaning of the speaker's message. In some cases, the meaning of the message will be clearly understood while in others it may be misinterpreted. Because these steps happen so quickly, we may not be consciously aware that they are happening. However, we can use this four-step model of communication to evaluate a couple's communication abilities, including where communication can break down for couples.

Step One – Internal and External Processors

Individuals vary in how thought out a message needs to be before they start to talk (Williams & Tappan, 1995). External processors are people who talk as they think and think as they talk. They are essentially saying their rough drafts out loud. External processors will often tell you that talking things out helps them think through things. Therefore, their ideas may evolve as they begin to talk. In contrast, internal processors are reluctant to say anything until they have carefully thought through things. They will usually not say anything until they have arrived at their final draft. They may even mentally rehearse what to say before saying anything out loud.

In terms of being an external or internal processor, one style is not better than another. However, conflict can arise between external and internal processors when they communicate, particularly if they are not aware of each other's different styles. For example, Rebecca (an external processor) begins to discuss with Devon (an internal processor) her thoughts on where they should go on vacation. Over the next several minutes, Rebecca suggests six different possible vacation locations, including reasons why each might be a good candidate. If you were to look at Devon's face, you might see a look of confusion. One moment it seems like Rebecca wants to go to Hawaii, but the next moment it appears that she wants to visit Disneyland in California instead. Seattle, Las Vegas, and Florida were also mentioned as possible options, as well as visiting her parents in Pennsylvania. He is not sure where she wants to go.

As an internal processor, Devon is assuming that you do not share what you are thinking until you have figured out your position. Devon is confused by Rebecca mentioning so many different vacation options and wonders why she does not simply state where she wants to go on vacation. Devon does not realize that she is an external processor, and that talking out loud about each of these options is helping her become clearer on what she really wants. Like other external processors, Rebecca's thoughts are evolving as she talks. That is why the external processor may say something later in the conversation that seems to contradict something said earlier in the conversation. What the external processor said a moment ago could be draft six, while what was said 5 minutes ago may have been the first or second draft. All this, of course, is confusing to the internal processor, who typically only shares the final draft with the listener.

Eventually, after discussing each option, Rebecca concludes that she wants to go to Disneyland for this year's vacation. She now turns to Devon and asks him what his opinion is on the matter. As an internal processor, Devon isn't ready to talk just yet because he has not had time to think through what he wants. Furthermore, he is still trying to understand the conflicting information he heard from Rebecca's multiple drafts. So, Devon mumbles, "I don't know." Rebecca interprets his noncommittal response as a sign that the topic is not important to him, so she becomes upset. Likewise, Devon may resent being put on the spot to articulate his opinion before he has had chance to sort through his thoughts.

If the couple differs in terms of being an internal or external processor, it can be helpful to assess how the couple manages their differences. First, does the couple recognize what each person is in terms of being an internal or external processor? If not, then educating the couple on this can be very helpful. For example, if Devon recognizes that Rebecca is an external processor, he may be more patient with her need to talk things out as a means of becoming clearer in her thinking. Likewise, Rebecca may not become as easily offended by Devon's reluctance to express his opinions right away if she understands his desire to think things out first before speaking as an internal processor.

Second, are both individuals explicit with their partner when they are externally or internally processing? For example, Rebecca might turn to Devon and say, "I have been trying to figure out what we should do for our vacation this year. It would help me if I could use you as a sounding board. Talking about it will help me be clearer on what I want to do." Conversely, Devon might reply when asked his opinion, "You have given me a lot to think about. You know how I like to think through things first before I talk. I need a minute to collect my thoughts before I speak." If Devon needs more time to internally process before sharing, then he would be wise to reassure Rebecca that he will be thinking about the topic and not simply ignoring or avoiding it.

Third, it may be helpful at times for external processors to do some external processing prior to talking to their partner. This may reduce the potential for information overload, particularly if their partner is an internal processor. Talking to someone else or journaling are ways individuals can do some preliminary external processing. Conversely, it may be helpful if internal processors make more of an effort to externalize some of their thinking. This helps partners feel like they are "in the loop," and perhaps feel more connected because they are getting more access to their mate's inner thoughts.

Step Two – Articulating the Message

Individuals sometimes need to be mindful about how they articulate their message, particularly if there is the potential for conflict to arise around the topic. How the speaker states their concern can influence how receptive the listener might be to the message. For example, if Arturo states to his partner Patricia, "You make me mad because you are such a slob," Patricia is likely to respond in a negative way.

This example reflects two potential problems that can arise in how individuals can communicate messages. One problematic strategy that individuals often use is to blame their partner for making them upset. This is evident when Arturo begins his sentence with "You" rather than "I." Patricia may immediately sense she is being criticized or blamed when Arturo begins his sentence in this way, which will make her defensive. Others cannot make you feel a particular way even though the other person's behavior can trigger an emotional response. For example, people will respond to the same situation in different ways. Some people will remain calm when a rude driver cuts them off, while others will respond with anger or rage. Therefore, Arturo should take responsibility for how he feels, such as stating, "I am mad because you are such a slob!"

Patricia is still not likely to respond well to Arturo's concern because he is also attacking her character rather than focusing on her behavior. No one is likely to respond well to a character assassination. However, Patricia might be more receptive if Arturo were to use an "I" statement and say, "I feel mad when you don't pick your clothes up off the bathroom floor." The formula for an "I" statement is to begin with the word "I," then individuals state the emotion they are feeling, followed by a brief description of the event or behavior that triggered the feeling. "I" statements are helpful because they encourage individuals to take responsibility for how they feel, as well as focus on the partner's offending behavior rather than possible character defects.

Individuals can also vary in how direct they are in expressing themselves. It may be helpful to assess how direct individuals are in expressing themselves, as well as factors that influence their level of directness. Some individuals may be reluctant to directly express themselves due to problems with assertiveness or fears of being rejected. However, it is also important to recognize that culture can play an important role in how direct individuals are in communicating. In some cultures, being direct is consider rude, and the listener is expected to use context (e.g., social cues, gestures) to discern the meaning behind the speaker's message.

Step Three – Message Received

Sometimes communication breaks down in receiving the message. The most common way that this can happen is if individuals are distracted. Distractions can come from a variety of sources. Events in our surroundings (e.g., the baby crying, the show on TV) can distract individuals from carefully listening to what their partner is saying. Individuals can also be distracted by what is going on inside their heads. For example, individuals may be preoccupied with the stressful events in their lives, which can make it difficult for them to focus on what their partner is saying.

Individuals may also not be attentive to what their partner is saying if they are formulating a rebuttal. Helping our clients become good listeners may require us to encourage them to suspend their agenda so that they can be open and receptive to what the speaker is saying.

As much as possible, it is important that couples remove both external and internal distractions when communicating with one another. Sometimes this can be a challenge, particularly for parents with young children. If external and internal distractions are difficult to eliminate, ideally the couple will postpone the conversation until a later time.

Be aware that some individuals may tune out the speaker, particularly if they anticipate that the speaker is delivering a negative message. For example, some teenagers are adept at tuning out what their parents are saying because they have little interest in hearing a lecture or criticism. However, adults can do this too. One client sheepishly admitted that he on occasion deliberately turn off his hearing aids to tune out his partner.

Problems with receiving the message can also occur due to hearing problems, even if individuals are trying to focus on what the speaker is saying. Hearing difficulties may cause individuals to miss parts of the message. Even missing one or two words can make it challenging to understand what the speaker has said. Some individuals may be reluctant to continually ask the speaker to repeat what they said, leaving the listener to guess or speculate what was said. Unfortunately, the listener may not accurately fill in the blanks, leading to an incorrect interpretation of the message.

Even if the listener has heard the message, speakers often appreciate evidence that the listener is actually listening. Therefore, it can be helpful to assess if individuals feel like they are receiving cues that their partner is paying attention and listening. For example, making direct eye contact can convey that the listener is paying attention. People also often provide short verbal cues that they are actively listening, such as saying "yes" or "uh-huh." Making a visible and deliberate effort to remove distractions such as turning the TV off or putting the phone down can also demonstrate that listening to what the person is saying is a priority. Accurately restating what the person has said or asking follow-up questions will also demonstrate that the listener is actively engaged in listening.

Be aware that gender differences may impact how men and women demonstrate they are listening (Tannen, 2007). Typically, women will directly face whomever they are listening to and make direct eye contact. In contrast, men are less likely to directly face the other person and make infrequent eye contact. Due to these differences, a woman may question whether the man is paying attention, even if he is actually listening. In addition to gender, cultural factors may also play a role in how much direct eye contact an individual is comfortable using.

Step Four – Decoding or Interpreting the Message

Even if individuals have accurately received the message, they are still left with the task of figuring out what the message means. The complexity of this task is illustrated by the fact that the same words spoken with a different tone can have very different meanings. "That's wonderful" could be an expression of excitement or happiness or an expression of disappointment if said in a sarcastic tone.

Several factors can make the task of accurately decoding the speaker's message difficult. Sometimes the speaker makes the task of interpreting the message a challenge. For example, the speaker may not provide enough information to decode the message. If your mate comes home and slams the door, you probably know they are upset. However, you may not know why your mate is upset. Is your mate upset with you or something else that happened? As noted earlier, an external processor may need time to verbalize things before the message is clear in their mind. This may lead to some initial confusion as to what the speaker is saying. The speaker may also send mixed messages if they feel ambivalent or conflicted about an issue. Finally, sometimes individuals may try to withhold sharing their feelings, but they still impact how the message is delivered. For example, Lakesha is upset that April is late for their lunch date, but she is trying to hide her anger. Yet, her body language and short responses to April's questions reflect that she is irritated. All these situations can make it challenging for the listener to accurately discern the meaning behind the speaker's message.

However, problems with interpreting the speaker's message can also rest with the listener. Obviously missing parts of the message due to lack of attention or hearing problems can result in misunderstanding (step three). However, even if the listener hears and sees everything the speaker communicates, it is still possible to misinterpret the message.

Individuals often use prior knowledge or experiences to help decode the meaning behind the other's words or actions. These previous experiences can create filters (Markman et al., 2010), which lead individuals to make assumptions about what the speaker is saying. For example, Corinne has a history of being overly critical of her husband Frank. As a result, Frank has developed a filter which leads him to interpret any negative comments by Corinne as personal criticism. In some cases, this filter may lead Frank to assume his wife is being critical of him even if that was not her intent.

Filters have the potential to distort how we view what our partner is saying, especially if we have developed an inaccurate filter. When this happens, the positive intent behind the speaker's message is lost, resulting in the message having a negative impact on the listener. Barbara was talking to her daughter Julie on the phone while her husband Sam was next to her in the car. Sam could sense from the tone of the conversation that his stepdaughter was sharing a problem with her mother. When Sam asked what was wrong, Barbara replied, "She is not your daughter." Sam felt rejected by this comment, which made him feel like he was not part of the family. He interpreted Barbara's comments through his filter that he was not lovable. When debriefing the incident in therapy, Barbara said she did not intend to communicate this message. Rather, she was trying to reassure Sam that he did not have to worry about it because she would take responsibility for it as her mother. In this example, both the ambiguous nature of the speaker's message and the listener's filter contributed to the couple's conflict.

For couples in distress, the filter often revolves around the theme of "You don't love or care about me." Like Sam and Barbara, the partner's actions get interpreted through this filter, even when this is not an accurate reflection of the speaker's intent. Individuals may not always understand why their words or actions had a negative impact on their partner because they know the intent behind their message was positive or benign. Helping couples be aware of each other's filters can sometimes prevent individuals from accidently triggering them. For example, if certain words or behaviors tend to trigger the filters, the partners can attempt to avoid saying or doing these things.

However, it also may be important to challenge filters, especially if they consistently lead to misinterpretations. Unfortunately, it is often difficult to eliminate filters once they are created because human beings tend to focus on information that supports their beliefs and ignore information that contradicts them. Thus, individuals may only see what they already believe. However, as an outside observer, you can help individuals identify and objectively evaluate the validity of their filters.

When challenging filters, it is sometimes helpful to determine how the filter developed in the first place. In Sam's case, his filter that he was unlovable was created before he met Barbara. His mother often reminded him that he was a "spitting image" of his father. Unfortunately, she despised Sam's father, which led Sam to conclude that he was not lovable in his mother's eyes. Sam's negative filter was reinforced by the conflict between he and Barbara. Barbara would frequently become impatient with Sam's misinterpretation of her actions as being uncaring. Unfortunately, her irritation would reinforce Sam's belief that Barbara did not really love or accept him.

Gender can be overlooked as an important context for understanding communication in heterosexual couples. Due to gender socialization, men and women may look at the same set of events through a different lens or filter, resulting in a different perspective of what occurred (Tannen, 2007). As result, misunderstandings can arise. Advice-giving is a good example of how different interpretations of the same behavior can occur. How do you interpret it when individuals give you advice? Are they taking an expert stance, demonstrating their superior knowledge or wisdom to you? Or is giving advice a way of showing that they care about you? Both views could be valid.

In general, women are primarily oriented toward looking at relationships through the lens of closeness or distance. Thus, they would be more likely to interpret someone giving them advice as an act of caring or evidence that they have a close relationship. In contrast, men are primarily oriented toward viewing relationships in terms of hierarchy, and typically want to avoid being in a dependent or one-down position relative to others. That is why men are often reluctant to seek help (e.g., to ask for directions) because it puts them in a dependent or one-down position relative to the other person. Thus, the man may not want unsolicited advice because it puts the advice-giver in a superior role relative to him. Tannen labels these different orientations between women and men as intimacy versus independence. To be clear, sometimes women are concerned with independence and men are concerned with intimacy. Thus, the lens that is used may depend upon the situation.

You will want to assess if these different orientations (intimacy versus independence) create misunderstandings or conflict in the couple's relationship. For example, Elaine would wait with anticipation for her husband Victor to come home from work. Upon his arrival, she would ask him several questions about his day. Elaine's questions were a bid for closeness, an attempt to start a conversation with her husband. Victor, however, resented the questions and would tend to withdraw. According to Victor, the questions made him feel like his wife was checking up on him, much like his mother had when he was a child. Therefore, Victor would withdraw to protect his autonomy, never recognizing that his wife's questions were actually a bid for connection or closeness.

Besides challenging filters, you can teach couples a variety of strategies to ensure they are accurately decoding each other's messages. For example, you can instruct them to look for cues that the partner does not feel understood, such as when they repeat all or parts of the message. In the earlier example of the couple discussing vacation possibilities, Rebecca tells Devon, "I was also thinking of going back home to Pennsylvania to visit my family for a week. We have not seen them since Christmas, so I would like to see them again. However, I would want to stay in a hotel so we could have some privacy." Devon responds, "So, you want to go see your parents?" Rebecca replies, "If we stay at a hotel." By repeating her statement about staying at a hotel, Rebecca is emphasizing that this is an important part of the message that she does not want to be lost.

Another strategy is to teach couples to do active listening, which essentially means the listener will repeat back to the speaker their interpretation of the message to obtain confirmation that this is what the speaker meant. In the above example, Devon would say, "So, you are thinking that seeing your parents might be an option to consider for vacation, but only if we stay in a hotel. Is that right?" Active listening is an essential skill taught in many communication skills programs. For example, active listening is an important element of the Speaker Listener Technique (Markman et al., 2010) in the Prevention and Relationship Education Program (PREP). Active listening not only confirms that the speaker's message has been accurately understood, but also signals to the speaker that the listener is paying attention and making a genuine effort to understand their point of view. This helps set a positive tone for the conversation, reducing the likelihood that conflict will escalate. It is important to remind clients that understanding the speaker's message is different from agreeing with what the speaker is saying. Through active listening, Devon can demonstrate that he understands Rebecca wants to consider vacationing with her family in Pennsylvania if they stay at a hotel. However, that does not mean that Devon agrees that this is the best vacation option.

Although correctly interpreting or decoding messages is critical to success in communication, being able to validate what the speaker is saying can also be important. Therefore, you should explore each partner's ability to offer validation as a listener. However, offering validation can be a challenge if the listener has a different perspective on the situation. In addition, it is especially difficult to offer validation when the speaker is upset with the listener. In these circumstances, it is easy for the listener to become defensive, especially if the listener did not do anything to intentionally make the speaker upset. However, being able to give some form of validation as a listener is especially helpful in these circumstances. For example, Alonzo is upset that Josephina did not call him to let him know she would be 30 minutes late for their date. Alonzo wonders if Josephina forgot about their date. Unfortunately, Josephina got caught in heavier than normal traffic and was unable to call Alonzo because her cellphone was not charged. Because Josephina did nothing intentionally to make Alonzo upset, she could easily become upset or defensive with Alonzo being mad at her. However, Josephina apologizes for being late and explains the circumstances. In addition, she validates Alonzo's feelings by saying that if she believed Alonzo had forgotten about a date they had planned, she would be upset too. Even if individuals don't fully agree with their partner, it is often possible to find a way to validate at least part of their experience as Josephina was able to do with Alonzo.

Communication and Intimacy

Being effective as a communicator is not only about *how* we communicate, but *what* we communicate. In this regard, communication is intertwined with intimacy, an important aspect of couple relationships. In fact, we often refer to individuals who are romantically involved as being in an *intimate* relationship.

Intimacy comes through revealing information about who we are. I heard a speaker at a conference refer to intimacy as "into me see." Intimacy is related to how private the information is. The most intimate disclosure is sharing something about ourselves with another person that we have never shared with anyone else before. Conversely, sharing our name with someone is not very intimate because this is information that is readily shared with hundreds of people. Thus, the fewer the people we have shared the information with, the more intimate the disclosure.

Intimate disclosures often require individuals to be vulnerable to some degree. When we reveal a private part of ourselves, there is always the risk that the other person will negatively judge or reject us. This is particularly true if the disclosure relates to something that we are not especially proud of, such as a weakness or a shortcoming. The potential for rejection can be a powerful deterrent for some to risk being intimate. However, being accepted for who we are, shortcomings and all, can deepen our bond or attachment to that individual. So, an intimate disclosure has the potential to strengthen the couple's relationship, but it also can create the potential for hurt or rejection.

You should assess if individuals have beliefs or past experiences that make it difficult for them to be intimate or vulnerable with their partner. For example, young boys are often taught this at an early age through messages like "big boys don't cry." As a result, men are often socialized to avoid being vulnerable or emotional, and instead are encouraged to be stoic or strong. Yet, ironically, the ability to make oneself vulnerable to another human being takes strength. Negative past experiences may also make it difficult for some individuals to risk trusting others. For example, childhood abuse or trauma may teach individuals that relationships are not safe, impacting their ability to be vulnerable with anyone, including their partner. Having one's trust violated in a significant way (e.g., an affair) in a past or present intimate relationship can also impact a person's willingness to be vulnerable.

Although conflict can create distance in a relationship, it can actually create the opportunity for greater connection if individuals risk being vulnerable with one another. When discussing an issue, there are three different ways to approach it. I refer to these as the "you," "we," and "me" approaches to addressing conflict. Typically, individuals will find that it is easier to resolve conflict if they use the "we" or "me" approach versus the "you" approach.

In the "you" approach, individuals focus on their partner, often pointing out what they are doing wrong. In this approach, individuals often begin with "you" statements. Curt is upset with the frequency with which he and Janelle have sex. An example of what Curt might say with the "you" approach is, "You don't seem interested in sex lately. What is the problem with you?" By focusing on his partner's shortcomings, Curt increases the likelihood that Janelle will become defensive.

The second approach is to focus on the relationship, which is the "we" level. This approach explores how the problem impacts the relationship or how the two partners relate around the problem. For example, Curt might say to Janelle, "I feel like our relationship could be stronger if we could have sex more often." Janelle is probably going to be more receptive to hearing this message versus being blamed for the problem.

The third or "me" approach is to focus on the meaning the issue has for the individual. This gives individuals the opportunity to share something more vulnerable about themselves, which can increase intimacy. For example, Curt might share, "I wish we could have sex more often. When we have sex, I feel connected and loved by you. When we don't have sex very often, I begin to worry that you don't love me." Janelle will likely be most receptive to this approach and may even try to reassure Curt that she does love him.

Using "I" statements encourages individuals to focus more on their own inner experience when talking to their partner about an issue. Thus, "I" statements have the potential to be more intimate disclosures and are therefore more consistent with the "me" approach versus the "you" approach.

"I" statements also include stating what emotion was triggered by the partner's actions. In terms of building an intimate connection, it is helpful to encourage individuals to think through which emotion they want to share with their partner. When individuals are upset, the emotion or feeling they often most easily access is anger. However, most people do not respond well to another person's anger. They will often respond with anger or withdraw to avoid experiencing the individual's anger. Both responses, however, can leave individuals feeling invalidated, and therefore perpetuate even more anger.

However, in many cases, individuals will often find that there are other emotions underneath their anger. In integrative behavioral couple therapy (IBCT), these are called the softer emotions (Christensen et al., 2015). In emotionally focused therapy (EFT), the vulnerable emotions that drive anger are called primary emotions (Johnson, 2004; Johnson, 2015). For example, perhaps anger is really being driven by feeling hurt by another person's actions or words. Individuals can also be angry with someone because their actions have triggered feelings of anxiety. For example, a parent might be mad at their child for not doing the assigned homework, but underneath the anger is a fear that the child will do poorly in school.

Helping individuals access and share the vulnerable feelings underneath the anger is more likely to elicit a positive response from their partner. Imagine that you encounter a young child who is lost or is hurt. The child is visibly upset and crying. How would you respond? If you are like most people, your instincts are to soothe, protect, or comfort the child. In a similar manner, if individuals share their hurt, fear, or sadness with their partner, then they are more likely to get a loving or compassionate response. Unfortunately, sometimes it feels safer to express anger rather than the more vulnerable emotions. It may be particularly difficult for men to share their more vulnerable emotions because they are frequently taught to be tough (e.g., big boys don't cry). As a result, men often channel many of their emotions through anger. Therefore, it can be important to assess a couple's ability to access and share their vulnerable emotions with one another. Some therapies like EFT (Johnson, 2004; Johnson, 2015) and IBCT (Christensen et al., 2015) provide therapists guidance on how to help couples do this.

Although individuals can foster intimacy by what they choose to disclose, partners can also encourage greater self-disclosure based on how they respond when their partner does share something. Therefore, you should assess whether both partners respond in a manner that facilitates or inhibits their partner from sharing. First, do both partners take an interest in the other person's experience? Individuals are likely to reveal more if their partner shows interest in what they are sharing.

Second, do individuals respond in a nonjudgmental manner? Making negative judgments when someone shares something that is vulnerable or intimate will shut down another person's willingness to share in the future.

Third, are individuals able to maintain curiosity with their partner? Curiosity can increase an individual's interest in what their partner is saying, as well as help individuals suspend making judgments. For example, curiosity may encourage an individual to consider questions like, "Why does my partner feel this way?" "What beliefs or fears are causing my partner to behave in this way?" Therefore, curiosity will motivate individuals to dig a bit deeper in seeking understanding of their partner, opening the possibilities up for a more intimate dialogue.

Finally, are both able to offer each other empathy or validation? Offering empathy is easier if individuals can connect what their partner is talking about to a situation similar to one that they have experienced. Jasmine was feeling extremely sad after the recent death of her mother. In an attempt to comfort Jasmine, her partner Marissa said, "One of the most difficult things I ever had to deal with was losing my mother to cancer. I know it must be devastating for you to lose your mother." Jasmine felt supported because Marissa was able to validate her feelings. Marissa was able to use her own experience regarding her mother's death to empathize with Jasmine's struggles of losing her mother. However, individuals need to be mindful that their partner's experience of the situation may be different from their own. The key to expressing empathy is to be able to see the event from the partner's frame of reference. Fortunately, encouraging individuals to listen carefully and be curious (without judgment) to better understand their partner's experience can be a form of validation.

Conclusion

Effective communication is a shared responsibility; both the speaker and the listener have an important role in determining the outcome. Table 3.1 summarizes key questions you can consider when evaluating a couple's communication. These questions will help you evaluate where a couple is doing well in terms of communication, and where they may need assistance to improve. Effective communication focuses on how couples talk about their problems. The next chapter on conflict resolution will focus on how couples actually go about addressing those problems.

Communication is also vital to a couple's intimacy. Building intimacy in a relationship requires that both be willing to take risks and be vulnerable. It also requires that each partner try to create a sense of safety so the other is willing to risk being intimate. If both people are willing to share their intimate selves, then this can help the relationship grow and evolve as each person changes.

Table 3.1 Assessment of Communication Skills

The following questions can help you assess a couple's areas of strengths and areas of growth with regard to communication:

1. Does each individual identify as an external or internal processor? If differences exist, how do they manage them? For example, do they make explicit to one another when they are externally or internally processing?

2. Do the individuals take responsibility for how they feel, or do they often blame each other for their feelings?

3. Do the individuals primarily focus on complaining about their partner's behaviors, or do they criticize each other's character?

4. How direct or indirect are both individuals in expressing themselves, and what factors (e.g., culture) influence the level of directness?

5. Does the couple struggle with external or internal distractions when communicating? What can the couple do to reduce these distractions?

6. Does either partner have difficulties with hearing that might impact communication?

7. How does the couple show each other that they are making an effort to listen to one another (e.g., eye contact, active listening)?

8. Are there any filters that negatively impact how individuals interpret the other's messages or actions? If so, where did these filters originate (e.g., family of origin, gender socialization)? How do these filters get triggered?

9. To what extent are both able to offer validation when listening to one another?

10. When discussing issues, to what extent do they focus on blaming the other person (the "you" perspective), the relationship (the "we" perspective), or sharing their own internal experience (the "me" perspective)?

11. To what extent do individuals confide in each other? If not, what are the barriers?

12. To what extent is each individual able to access and share their more vulnerable emotions with one another?

13. Are individuals able to respond in a manner that makes it safe for their partner to be vulnerable (e.g., is nonjudgmental, shows interest, is curious, offers empathy or validation)?

4

CONFLICT RESOLUTION

Conflict is an inevitable part of any intimate relationship. It is often believed that the healthiest couples experience the least conflict. However, some couples who experience little conflict may actually be avoiding issues that need to be addressed. Research suggests that the best predictor of how well a couple will do in the future is not the absence of conflict, but how they handle it when it arises (Gottman, 1999). Couples who learn to manage conflict effectively will enjoy healthier relationships. In contrast, couples that handle conflict poorly are at significant risk for relationship dissatisfaction and ending their relationship. This chapter will help you assess a couple's ability to effectively manage conflict in order to minimize the destructive effects that it can have on a relationship.

The Warning Signs for Poorly Handled Conflict

John Gottman is a researcher who has extensively studied married couples for many years. In his research, Gottman has uncovered strong predictors

DOI: 10.4324/9781003161967-4

of divorce. One of the strongest predictors of divorce is when couples engage in criticism, contempt, defensiveness, and stonewalling during conflict. These four behaviors have been called the Four Horsemen of the Apocalypse (J. M. Gottman & J. S. Gottman, 2015; J. S. Gottman & J. M. Gottman, 2015). Therefore, it is important that you assess for the Four Horsemen, which are described next.

Criticism is the first horseman and occurs when individuals attack their partner's character rather than simply complain about their behavior. "I" statements (see Chapter 3) are the antidote to criticism because they encourage individuals to focus their complaint on the partner's behavior rather than attacking their character.

The second horseman is *contempt*, which is manifested when individuals view themselves as superior to their partner and belittle them. Contempt can be evident in the words individuals say or through their nonverbal communication. For example, rolling one's eyes can be a form of contempt, which essentially communicates to the partner, "How could I have married someone so stupid!" The antidote to contempt is for individuals to build respect for their partner (J. M. Gottman & J. S. Gottman, 2015). One way to cultivate this respect is for individuals to get into the habit of expressing appreciation to their partner for their positive qualities. Developing this habit means making a consistent and conscious effort to notice the things one's partner does that reflect these positive qualities. Over time, expressing appreciation for one's partner will help restore respect in the relationship and reduce contempt.

Individuals can experience *defensiveness*, the third horseman, when they feel criticized or attacked. Individuals are reluctant to take responsibility or ownership for a problem when they become defensive. They will make excuses for their behavior, or they may turn the tables and blame the other person for the problem. The antidote to defensiveness is to take responsibility, even for part of the problem.

Finally, the fourth horseman is *stonewalling*. Stonewalling occurs when individuals become overwhelmed by the conflict and essentially shut down. Stonewalling individuals are simply waiting out the argument and are emotionally checked out. The best way to prevent stonewalling is to prevent the conflict from escalating to the point where individuals become flooded with negative emotions, which is the focus of the next section.

Flooding

As couples discuss their issues, conflict can escalate from a minor disagreement to a major fight or argument. This is especially true if the couple engages in the Four Horsemen previously described. As a couple's conflict begins to escalate, one or both partners can become flooded with negative emotions, also called diffuse physiological arousal (J. M. Gottman & J. S. Gottman, 2015).

When individuals start to become flooded, several changes happen. Physiologically, individuals will notice that their heart rate goes up. Stress hormones begin to flow through the body. The body responds as if it is under attack, often leading individuals to respond with a flight or fight response. Individuals who have a fight response will continue to pursue the argument, whereas individuals who have a flight response will withdraw or emotionally shut down (e.g., stonewalling). A couple's conflict pattern will depend upon each partner's predominant way of coping with flooding. For example, two people who typically develop a fight response may find that their arguments quickly escalate and can become intense. If one partner typically has a fight response and the other a flight response, then you will see a pattern where one is continuing to pursue the argument while the other is emotionally shutting down or withdrawing. Unfortunately, the withdrawing partner's reluctance to discuss the issue can make the other partner more upset, leading him or her to pursue with greater intensity. This, in turn, only makes the withdrawing partner want to withdraw even more. You can also have couples who mutually withdraw because they both have a flight response when flooded. These couples may adopt a conflict-avoidant stance when facing issues.

Flooding also leads individuals to think more negatively. They view both the situation and their partner in a much more negative light. For example, Susanna discussed how she wanted to improve her relationship with her mother-in-law in therapy. When she wasn't flooded, Susanna could articulate reasons why this would be helpful, including reducing some friction in her marriage. However, as Susanna remembered hurtful comments her mother-in-law had made, she began to get flooded with negative emotions. She soon switched to seeing her mother-in-law as the "devil incarnate," and emphatically stated that she wanted nothing to do with the woman.

Couples are most likely to say or do something that is destructive to the relationship when they are flooded. For example, some individuals may express contempt for their partner during a fight or argument. Others may threaten divorce in the heat of the moment. Therefore, it is important that couples recognize when they are becoming flooded so they can exit these interactions as quickly as possible to minimize the harm done to their relationship.

Therefore, it is helpful that you explore what flooding looks like for each partner. There may be a number of signs that individuals can look for that signal they are getting flooded. Some people will sense it in their body due to the physiological changes (e.g., increased heart rate). Some individuals begin to raise their voice when they get flooded. Individuals can also slip into all or nothing thinking, such as saying, "You always . . . " or "You never . . . " when flooded. Flooding can also make individuals more rigid in their thinking. Couples can also use pulse oximeters to measure their pulse rate and oxygen concentrations to signal when they are becoming flooded (J. M. Gottman & J. S. Gottman, 2015).

When couples become flooded, it is best to stop interacting by taking a time out (J. M. Gottman & J. S. Gottman, 2015; Markman et al., 2010). Some couples recognize the need to take a time out, but they do so in an ineffective manner. Thus, it is important to assess if a couple knows when and how to take a time out. Does the couple clearly communicate when they are taking a time out? One woman recognized when she was becoming too upset to think or act clearly, so she would take a time out. However, she would simply walk away from her husband rather than make explicit that she was taking a time out. As a result, her husband felt like she was ignoring him or blowing him off, which further infuriated him. It is also important to ask if both honor the time out when one is called. Or does one or both of the individuals continue to pursue the argument? During a time out, both partners will ideally go to separate places to avoid interacting with one another until they are no longer flooded. Also, does the couple allow enough time to calm down before they resume talking about the issue? A time out needs to be at least 20 minutes because it takes individuals this long to physiologically calm down once they become flooded (Gottman, 1999). To avoid restarting the conversation too quickly, one couple would put a large ice cube on the kitchen table and were not allowed to speak to one another until the ice cube had completely melted. Some individuals may require more than 20 minutes to calm down, especially if they ruminate about the conflict. As a result, it is also important to assess what strategies each person uses to soothe themselves when they become flooded (J. S. Gottman & J. M. Gottman, 2015). For some couples, you may need to teach them some ways to self-soothe (e.g., exercising, meditating, journaling, listening to music) so they can de-escalate after being flooded. Finally, does the couple revisit the issue once both parties have calmed down? If not, one or both may use a time out as a way to avoid talking about the issue altogether. Many couples find it helpful to have an agreement that whoever asks for the time out is also responsible for restarting the conversation. When restarting the conversation, couples may want to use communication skills like the Speaker Listener Technique (Markman et al., 2010) to prevent flooding from occurring again.

Emotional Dysregulation During Conflict

Poor communication (see Chapter 3) and using the Four Horsemen can contribute to conflict escalation and flooding. In some cases, individuals who become flooded can lose control of their emotions and become emotionally dysregulated. Individuals who become emotionally dysregulated may become verbally or physically abusive toward their partner, or they may threaten to harm or kill themselves. Therefore, it is important to assess for factors that can contribute to individuals becoming emotional dysregulated during conflict.

You should assess if substance use contributes to individuals becoming emotionally dysregulated during conflict. Many couples experience their worst conflicts when under the influence of alcohol or drugs because these can significantly lower inhibitions. Therefore, couples should be warned against talking about issues if either of them is under the influence of alcohol or drugs. In some cases, one or both individuals may need a referral for substance abuse treatment.

You should also assess if mental illness contributes to emotional dysregulation in either partner. For example, couples where one person has borderline personality disorder can experience escalated conflict (Fruzzetti & Payne, 2015). The couple can fall into a vicious cycle where the individual with borderline personality disorder becomes emotionally dysregulated due to an incident, which leads the partner to respond in an invalidating manner. The partner's invalidating response creates further hurt and emotional dysregulation for the individual with borderline personality disorder, which continues to perpetuate the cycle. Problems with emotional dysregulation also can occur in individuals with other mental health disorders, such as bipolar disorder, PTSD, ADHD, or intermittent explosive disorder. A couple therapy approach based on dialectical behavior therapy (DBT) has been developed (Fruzzetti & Payne, 2015) for couples where emotional dysregulation is a significant concern.

Intimate Partner Violence

When working with couples, it is important to always assess for intimate partner violence or relationship aggression (Stith et al., 2020). This is especially true for couples where one or both are prone to becoming emotionally dysregulated. In Chapter 2, the importance of assessing for intimate partner violence using an assessment instrument (e.g., Revised Conflict Tactics Scale) and during individual interviews was stressed. This is consistent with best practice, which is to evaluate for intimate partner violence at the beginning of therapy using more than one technique (Bradford, 2010). If intimate partner violence is uncovered, then further assessment will be needed to determine the severity and nature of the violence. This assessment will inform whether or not conjoint work can be done.

Intimate or patriarchal terrorism is one type of violence described in the literature (Greene & Bogo, 2002). In intimate terrorism, the perpetrator uses violence to exert control over the partner. Men are typically the perpetrators of this type of violence. Conjoint therapy is contraindicated when intimate terrorism exists, and both partners should be referred to individual therapy.

Situational couple violence is another type of intimate partner violence (Greene & Bogo, 2002). For these couples, partners will intermittently become physical with one another, especially if an argument escalates in intensity. In couple situational violence, acts of violence are typically less severe and women are just as likely as men to use some form of physical aggression. In contrast to intimate terrorism, violence in these couples is not characterized by a pervasive pattern of control.

Conjoint therapy may be feasible in the case of couple situational violence, whereas it is clearly contraindicated when intimate terrorism is present (Stith et al., 2020). Therefore, it is important to assess what type of violence is occurring. Greene and Bogo (2002) suggest four factors that can distinguish between the two. First, you should assess the motivation behind the violence. For intimate terrorism, the motivation for the violence (or threat of violence) is control, which is not true for situational couple violence. Second, you should assess for other control tactics, which is indicative of intimate terrorism. Perpetrators of intimate terrorism often use other means of control like restricting finances or isolating the individual from others. Third, you should assess the impact of the violence. Because violence in intimate terrorism tends to be more severe, there is a greater likelihood of a negative impact on the person's health, relationships, occupational functioning, and emotional well-being. Finally, victims of intimate terrorism fear their partner, whereas this is often not the case for situational couple violence.

Bograd and Mederos (1999) provide additional guidance on how to evaluate if conjoint therapy is feasible. They suggest that several conditions should be met before one can safely do conjoint therapy. These conditions include: (a) both partners agree to participate in therapy without any coercion; (b) there are no fears of retribution; (c) violence is infrequent and mild with no physical injuries; (d) there are no risk factors for lethality (e.g., choking, threatening with a gun); (e) use of psychological abuse is infrequent and mild; (f) the aggressor assumes responsibility for their behavior and is willing to address it; and (g) the aggressor makes an ongoing commitment to contain explosive feelings. Assuming conjoint therapy is not clearly contraindicated, then current research supports the effectiveness of couple therapy for treating intimate partner violence (Stith et al., 2020).

If you uncover intimate partner violence, you should be mindful of the legal and ethical considerations. For example, an elder abuse report may be required if the victim is considered an elder by state standards. If the couple has children, then you should assess for possible child abuse and the need to make a report. In California, therapists are mandated to make a child abuse report if the children are in harm's way as a result of domestic violence. For example, a child who attempts to stop the violence between their parents is at risk for being physically injured.

California also permits therapists to file a child abuse report if children are emotionally harmed by witnessing domestic violence even if they are not at risk for being physically injured. In addition to possible reporting responsibilities, the therapist has an ethical responsibility to work with the couple to develop a safety plan and help them take the necessary steps to eliminate future violence.

Protective Factors in Managing Conflict

The Prevention and Relationship Education Program (PREP) (Markman et al., 2010) offers several ground rules to help couples manage conflict in their relationship. These ground rules, described next, point to various strategies that couples can use to protect the relationship from conflict. Therefore, it can be helpful to assess if couples use any of these strategies. If not, then teaching couples these skills can enhance their ability to handle conflict when it arises.

First, PREP recommends that couples use the Speaker Listener Technique described in Chapter 3 whenever they are struggling with communication. Because the Speaker Listener Technique helps ensure that each partner feels heard, emotions are less likely to escalate, leading to a more productive conversation. Couples might use the Speaker Listener Technique once they notice that the conversation is starting to get a little heated, or at the beginning of the conversation if the topic has historically led to an argument.

Second, PREP recommends that couples separate their problem discussion from problem solving. This is consistent with the Gottman approach of seeking understanding before persuasion (J. M. Gottman & J. S. Gottman, 2015). It is important that both partners feel like the other person understands their perspective. This will likely include why the issue is important to each person and what each person's needs are around the issue. Once this happens, the couple can transition to finding a solution that will be agreeable to both.

Third, individuals always have the right to tell their partner that it is not a good time to talk about an issue. Timing is important. If individuals are already stressed, irritable, hungry, or tired, then conflict is more likely to emerge during the discussion. Couples should also refrain from talking about issues when either is under the influence of alcohol or drugs. Individuals can check with their partner to assess their receptiveness to talking about an issue, such as asking, "I want to talk about our financial situation. Is this a good time to talk?" If not, the partner can request that the conversation be postponed until a later time. If the partner requests to postpone the conversation, then they will ideally re-initiate the conversation when the timing is better.

Fourth, PREP recommends that couples protect time in their relationship for fun, friendship, support, and sensuality. Couples not only need this time to enjoy one another, but it may also influence how they interact when handling conflict. There is evidence that building positive interactions outside of conflict may encourage more positive interactions when a couple is in conflict (J. M. Gottman & J. S. Gottman, 2015). Building a strong relationship outside of conflict can help create positive sentiment override (Gottman, 1999). When positive sentiment override exists, the overall positive feelings about the partner or relationship will override the negative event in the moment. For example, we will be more likely to give our partner the benefit of the doubt if they are irritable and simply attribute it to them having a bad day. In contrast, if negative sentiment override exists, we will have a "chip on our shoulder" and respond negatively to our partner's irritability. Rather than give our partner the benefit of the doubt, we will see their irritability as further evidence that the partner is a jerk, selfish, mean, or some other negative attribute. Therefore, it will be important to assess the extent to which the couple has developed a strong relationship outside of conflict (see Chapter 7 on caring). Enhancing caring in the couple's relationship will facilitate the couple being more positive during conflict, as well as promote positive sentiment override.

When couples set aside time to enjoy each other, they need to be careful not to discuss issues during this time. For example, couples with children who rarely get time to themselves may be tempted to talk about issues on their date, but this will interfere with their ability to enjoy one another.

Fifth, PREP advises couples to have weekly business meetings. By having weekly business meetings, the couple can then protect their dates or time together without having to focus on issues. Weekly business meetings also help couples who have a tendency to avoid issues. If the couple avoids issues, then tension can build up over time. A seemingly small incident can trigger a big conflict because the incident becomes the proverbial "straw that broke the camel's back." Weekly meetings encourage couples to address issues on a consistent basis rather than allowing them to accumulate and become explosive or overwhelming. Jennifer and Dave said that they had fewer arguments when they adopted this approach. In addition, Dave liked that he knew when issues were going to be raised rather than being caught off guard by Jennifer's concerns, which allowed him to be less defensive.

Types of Problems That Can Create Conflict

Through his research, John Gottman has observed that two types of problems exist which can lead to couple conflict, which he calls resolvable and perpetual problems (Gottman & Silver, 1999). Resolvable problems, once successfully addressed, do not have to be dealt with again. For example, Zia and Tyrone are debating where to go on their honeymoon. They initially can't agree on where to go; however, the couple eventually decides on a destination. The couple enjoys a wonderful honeymoon, and the issue is resolved for them.

In contrast, perpetual problems will continually arise in the couple's relationship. In fact, Gottman's research suggests that 69% of conflict is a result of a perpetual problem (J. M. Gottman & J. S. Gottman, 2015). Perpetual problems exist in all couple relationships, and they arise because there will be some fundamental way in which the partners differ in terms of temperament, values, or preferences. Diane and Jarod often have conflict over their finances due to their different orientations toward money. Diane has a strong need for future financial security. As a result, she wants the couple to be very careful in how much money they spend in the present so that they can put a significant portion of their earnings into savings. Jarod has more of a "live for today" mentality, which is evident in his desire to spend money on things that provide him enjoyment in the present. As a result, conflict often occurs if Jarod spends money on something that Diane feels is unnecessary or frivolous.

The approach to handling resolvable and perpetual problems is different, so it is important that you help the couple determine the extent to which the issue is resolvable or perpetual in nature. For resolvable problems, your goal is to help the couple identify what changes can be made to remedy the issue. A problem-solving model like the one used in

PREP (Markman et al., 2010) may help couples get unstuck when facing a difficult resolvable problem. In the PREP model, couples agree upon the problem they are trying to solve, brainstorm possible solutions, and then agree to specific solutions to try, which often requires compromise.

For perpetual problems, acceptance is the key. For example, Diane and Jarod will need to accept that the other person has a different orientation to money that is not likely to change. Perpetual problems require couples to find constructive ways to accept and live with their differences rather than destructively arguing over them. For example, Jarod may need to agree that a certain amount of money must be put into savings, much like paying other bills, in order to make Diane happy. Likewise, Diane may need to accept that Jarod needs a certain amount of discretionary income for his "toys." The couple can create their budget taking both of these considerations into account. The difference in resolvable and perpetual problems is captured by what is known as the serenity prayer – *"Change what you can change, accept what you cannot, and have the wisdom to know the difference between the two."* Through your assessment, you and the couple can obtain the wisdom to know the difference between the two.

When helping a couple manage a perpetual problem, it can be helpful to assess what factors encourage acceptance and what factors interfere with it. The following questions will help you uncover these factors. First, does the couple's differences touch upon an emotional sensitivity or vulnerability that the individuals may have (Christensen et al., 2015)? For example, when Jarod spends money on his "toys," this often taps into Diane's anxiety about the future. The more anxious she is about the future, the more likely she is to respond in anger to what she sees as his irresponsible spending. Uncovering and addressing these vulnerabilities can facilitate acceptance.

Second, to what extent does each appreciate the value of the other's difference? For example, Jarod's philosophy of enjoying life in the moment is a nice counterbalance to Diane's worrying about the future. Likewise, Jarod appreciates Diane's desire to save money for the couple's future security. He recognizes that without Diane's prompting, it would be difficult for him to save money for emergencies or retirement. Asking couples about what initially attracted them to one another can sometimes uncover the value they once saw in their differences. For example, Diane liked Jarod's ability to have fun when they first dated, while Jarod liked how grounded Diane seemed to be as a person.

Third, is each individual able to understand how their partner's behavior fits within the context of their life? Jarod grew up in a relatively affluent family, so he never worried about money. In contrast, Diane grew up in a low-income family. In one session, Diane shared memories of how her father was inconsistently employed as a construction worker, which created periods where the family struggled financially. Learning more about Diane's upbringing helped Jarod be more understanding about her anxiety around finances and her wanting to be secure in the future.

Fourth, does each partner understand the deeper meaning of the other's behavior? For example, Jarod is a paraplegic and worries that health issues related to his paraplegia will shorten his lifespan. One day Jarod tells Diane that he is not sure why he should save so much money for a future that he might not see. He asks her if it is so bad if he wants to spend money on a larger television so he can enjoy his life now. Likewise, Diane shares her fear about the future, including whether the couple will have enough money to live on at retirement. Sharing these fears with one another did not change either person's philosophy around money, but it helped each be more accepting of the other's desires around how to allocate their money. Therapists can consider using the dream-within-conflict exercise to get at the deeper meaning for each partner (J. S. Gottman & J. M. Gottman, 2015).

Conflict and Vicious Cycles

One of the things that can make conflict difficult to resolve is if the couple finds themselves trapped in a vicious cycle. When this occurs, how each person responds to the other's actions perpetuates the conflict. Each person's efforts to get the other to change feeds the cycle. The two couples described next provide two illustrations of how couples may find themselves locked in a vicious cycle.

Paul and Madeline are caught in a classic distance-pursue pattern. Madeline wants more emotional connection with Paul, so she pushes for more closeness and time with him. However, Paul does not feel the same need for emotional closeness, so he resists Madeline's pressure to spend more time together by withdrawing. He also dislikes how Madeline can become angry and critical over the amount of time he devotes to her. Unfortunately, Paul's withdrawal or distancing makes Madeline feel hurt and strengthens her desire to reconnect. Thus, she pursues Paul more intensely by becoming angry or critical, accusing him of not caring about her or their relationship.

Cheyenne is mad at Denise because she did not search for a new job again today. Denise has been unemployed for 3 months, but she has not invested much time in looking for new employment recently. It also appears that she has not done any of the chores or errands that Cheyenne requested that she do. From Cheyenne's perspective, it appears that Denise has wasted another day. Cheyenne gets angry with her and slips into contempt by putting her down for her laziness. Denise does not protest much because she believes she should have tried harder today to search for work. However, she has been struggling with depression since losing her job 3 months ago. She finds it very difficult to get motivated to do anything due to her depression. In addition, losing her job has greatly undercut her confidence, leading her to avoid seeking a new job because she fears she will not be successful. Cheyenne's anger and criticisms only reinforce Denise's struggles with depression and self-doubt, further reducing her motivation to seek employment or do household chores.

Identifying and disrupting dysfunctional interactional patterns could be viewed as a common factor in treating couples (Davis et al., 2012; Karam & Blow, 2020). Therefore, one of the most important things you can do to help couples is to help them identify and interrupt their vicious cycles. Vicious cycles can be uncovered both through observation and clinical questioning. It is not uncommon for couples to act out their cycle in session, particularly if they become upset discussing a key issue. Some couples may be able to give you clues to their cycle when asked, although many cannot. However, you may be able to piece the cycle together by identifying the triggers for each person, why their partner's behavior bothers each of them, and how they each respond. Putting these elements into the proper sequence will often reveal the couple's vicious cycle.

For example, Kylie notices that Jasper is withdrawn. Kylie assumes, "Jasper does not care about me." Naturally, this leads Kylie to feel hurt and rejected. Kylie responds by criticizing Jasper for not caring more about her. Kylie's criticism triggers a negative response in Jasper, who thinks to himself, "I can never make Kylie happy." This thought, in turn, makes Jasper feel inadequate as a partner. Jasper copes with these feelings by withdrawing, which naturally only reinforces Kylie feeling like Jasper does not care, thereby perpetuating the vicious cycle.

How you attempt to alter the cycle may depend upon the theory that you use. A cognitively oriented therapist will attempt to challenge the meaning that each partner attributes to the other's behavior. For example, the therapist working with Kylie and Jasper might help Kylie recognize that Jasper withdraws not because he does not care, but because he feels inadequate as a partner. This new understanding of Jasper's behavior could help make Kylie less reactive when Jasper withdraws. In contrast, a therapist who likes EFT or IBCT might try to interrupt the cycle by helping Kylie and Jasper access and share their more vulnerable emotions. This, in turn, will likely lead the partner to respond in a different way, interrupting the cycle. When Kylie shares how scared she is that Jasper no longer loves her when he withdraws, he is shocked and surprised. Instead of withdrawing, Jasper immediately begins to comfort her by telling her how much she means to him.

Couples do not exist in a vacuum and are shaped by forces outside their relationship. Therefore, it is important to assess how these contextual or sociocultural factors might be influencing the couple's dynamics. In the example of Kylie and Jasper, contextual factors have a significant impact on the couple's cycle. Due to a downturn in the economy, Jasper's work hours have been reduced, creating some financial strain for the couple. While Kylie is grateful that Jasper still has his job and believes the financial stressors will be temporary, Jasper feels like he is failing in his role as the primary breadwinner for his family, which is important to his identity as a male. Kylie's criticism of him not caring enough only adds to these insecurities. Furthermore, Jasper is reluctant to directly disclose that the reason he has been more withdrawn lately is due to his anxiety about being an adequate provider. His gender socialization reinforces that men should be stoic and strong rather than vulnerable. The next chapter will examine in more detail how to include a sociocultural perspective in the assessment of couples.

Conclusion

This chapter has explored conflict in intimate relationships. Although conflict is unavoidable and has the potential to damage relationships, it can also serve as a catalyst for growth if handled properly. Therefore, you should assess the extent to which the couple can effectively manage conflict (see Table 4.1). Signs of poorly handled conflict include the presence of the Four Horsemen (criticism, defensiveness, contempt, stonewalling), regularly becoming flooded with negative emotions, and intimate partner violence. In addition to looking at risk factors for handling conflict poorly, the chapter also discussed positive strategies that couples can use to protect the relationship from conflict (e.g., time outs, PREP ground rules).

The chapter also examined how conflict can arise from problems that are either resolvable or perpetual in nature. Acceptance is the key to effectively managing perpetual problems in relationships. Therefore, this chapter outlined multiple factors that either facilitate or are barriers to acceptance. Finally, the chapter discussed the importance of identifying negative interactional patterns or vicious cycles that need to be interrupted to help couples develop more satisfying relationships, including the contextual factors that shape these interactions.

Table 4.1 Assessing How Couples Handle Conflict

Every relationship must contend with problems and the potential for conflict. The following questions can help you assess a couple's ability to handle and address problems and conflict in their relationship:

1. Overall, how well does the couple seem to handle conflict? Is there evidence of the Four Horsemen (criticism, defensiveness, contempt, stonewalling)? Is the couple prone to getting flooded when discussing issues?

2. What is the couple's pattern when flooded (e.g., fight-fight pattern, fight-flight pattern, flight-flight pattern)? What do they say or do when flooded?

3. Is the couple able to recognize the signs they are getting flooded?

4. Does the couple know how to effectively take a time out when flooded (e.g., ask for a time out, know how to self-soothe, restart the conversation at a later time)?

5. Does one or both partners struggle with emotional dysregulation, especially during conflict? If so, what is the underlying reason (e.g., mental illness, substance use)?

6. Is there intimate partner violence in the relationship? If so, is it intimate terrorism or situational couple violence? Is conjoint therapy contraindicated?

7. Does the couple use any of the PREP ground rules to protect the relationship from conflict (e.g., use Speaker-Listener technique, separate problem discussion from problem solving, be aware of timing when discussing issues, strengthen the relationship outside of conflict, regularly address issues through weekly business meetings)?

8. Does the couple have a clear understanding of what issues are resolvable problems and which are perpetual problems? For perpetual problems, what are the underlying differences (e.g., difference in personality, values, philosophy in life)?

9. To what extent does the couple accept their differences related to their perpetual problem(s)? What factors facilitate or interfere with their ability to have acceptance?

    a. Does the perpetual problem tap into an emotional sensitivity for either partner?

    b. What potential value do the differences hold for the couple?

    c. How does each person's behavior make sense in the context of their life? For example, do differences in family upbringing, culture, religion, or gender explain the differences?

    d. What is the deeper meaning of each person's behavior?

10. What is the couple's vicious cycle? What contextual factors impact how the couple relate to one another?

5

CULTURE

It is important to assess cultural factors due to the variety of ways in which they can impact couples. The most obvious example of how culture may play a role is if the partners belong to two different races or ethnicities. However, culture can be defined in other ways, and may also include other aspects such as religion, nationality, socioeconomic status, gender, or sexual orientation. In some cases, couples may have differences in multiple areas. For example, Daphne is a White, Southern Baptist woman from Alabama. She recently married Daha, a Hindu man who was raised in India until he moved to the United States in his early 20s. Daphne and Daha have several cultural differences, including race/ethnicity, gender, nationality, and religion. All these differences have the potential to influence the couple's relationship in some way.

This chapter will look at how incorporating culture into couple assessment is important in three ways. First, the chapter will examine intercultural couples like Daha and Daphne. This section will explore how to assess the possible impact of cultural differences on a couple's relationship,

DOI: 10.4324/9781003161967-5

as well as strategies couples might use to address these differences. Second, it is important to consider the sociocultural context in which all couples are embedded. Larger systems can impact couples in numerous ways. For example, internalized messages regarding gender can influence how a couple relates to one another. The sociocultural context can also play an important role in the distribution of power within intimate relationships. Third, cultural factors can impact the extent to which a couple's relationship is accepted by others. For example, an intercultural couple like Daphne and Daha could potentially struggle with gaining acceptance from their extended families and others.

Cultural Differences Between Partners

For a couple like Daha and Daphne, several cultural differences will obviously need to be navigated. Although cultural differences might be readily apparent for a couple like Daha and Daphne, sometimes two people who at first glance appear to be the same may actually have significant cultural differences if explored a little deeper. For example, Luis and Delores both identify as Hispanic, but the two have very different levels of acculturation. Likewise, both Peyton and Terence identify as being Catholic. However, Peyton is very devout and closely follows the teachings of the Catholic Church, whereas Terence rarely attends church and disagrees with many of the church teachings.

Potential Impact of Cultural Differences

During assessment, it is important to explore how cultural differences might present challenges and opportunities for the couple. Described next are some of the more common ways that cultural differences can impact couples. However, the description is not exhaustive, so it is important that you maintain a curious stance when exploring the impact of cultural differences on couples.

Communication

Communication is one area that can be impacted by cultural differences (Singh et al., 2020; Tili & Barker, 2015). For some couples, language differences become the first communication barrier they must overcome. Chandler met Maritza when he travelled to Ecuador for a month-long mission trip. The couple fell in love despite Chandler's limited ability to speak Spanish and Maritza speaking only Spanish. Not surprisingly, communication was a challenge for the couple because neither spoke the other person's language fluently.

Language abilities can also impact the couple's power dynamics by putting one person in a more dependent position. When the couple lived together in the United States, Maritza's limited ability to speak English made her reliant upon Chandler to translate in many situations. In addition, she had limited job opportunities due to her inability to speak English fluently, which made her more economically dependent upon Chandler.

Challenges can also arise for some couples if their cultures contribute to different communication styles, particularly around expressing emotions (Kellner, 2009; Maynigo, 2017). For example, Sofia was raised in an Italian American family where the expression of emotions, including anger, was not uncommon. In contrast, Hideki was raised in a traditional Japanese family that was reserved in expressing emotions. Although Hideki was born in the United States, his parents were raised in Japan and impressed on Hideki the need to avoid strong displays of emotion. Sofia experienced Hideki's lack of emotional expressiveness as evidence that he did not care about her, which would only make her upset. In contrast, Hideki found it difficult to deal with Sofia's expression of strong emotions, and he would withdraw or accuse her of being overly emotional, which only escalated her emotions.

Family Connections

Intercultural couples can experience challenges when it comes to navigating their relationships with extended family (Bustamante et al., 2011; Maynigo, 2017). Cultures can vary in how individuals are expected to balance their individual needs with the needs of others. The American culture has been characterized as more individualistic, with a tradition of valuing personal autonomy and independence. In contrast, individuals from collectivist cultures are more willing to set aside their personal needs for the collective well-being of their extended family. In collectivist cultures, loyalty and maintaining a strong connection to extended family are extremely important. Individuals who are not from a collectivist culture may view the extended family as overly involved. For example, when Patrick and Mariana came into therapy, their two primary issues were Patrick's use of alcohol and Mariana's relationship with her family. Patrick was raised in a rural Kansas community and left home right after graduating from high school to join the military. Patrick described his family as caring but not emotionally close. Patrick talked to his parents and brother by phone once a month. Mariana was raised in a traditional Mexican family, who lived less than an hour away from the couple. Mariana talked to her mother almost daily. In addition, many weekends were devoted to attending family gatherings or celebrations for Mariana's extended family. Although Patrick initially liked the warmth and connection he observed in Mariana's extended family, over time he began to resent the frequent obligation to attend family events on weekends. Patrick also complained that Mariana shared too much about the couple's problems with her family, and he expressed frustration that Mariana's family was over-involved in what he felt was their private life. Mariana felt caught in the middle between her husband's desire to spend less time with her family and her own feelings of loyalty toward her family. She also felt like she needed the support of her family as she struggled with Patrick's substance use. Patrick and Mariana obviously learned very different blueprints from their families on the role and importance of extended family, which was a source of conflict for the couple.

Different Values

Differences in cultural backgrounds can also contribute to couples having different values (Maynigo, 2017; Singh et al., 2020), which may have implications for the relationship. For example, Ryan and Noelle had very different beliefs about premarital sex. Noelle, a very devout Catholic, felt that sex before marriage was not appropriate. Ryan, who was agnostic, believed that it was acceptable for a couple to have sex before marriage if they loved one another. The couple was clearly at odds over their conflicting values regarding premarital sex.

Parenting

Cultural differences can also create challenges for couples when it comes to parenting (Bhugun, 2017; Blount & Young, 2015; Bustamante et al., 2011; Crippen & Brew, 2007; Maynigo, 2017). Couples may find that they have different beliefs about parenting practices due to their different cultural backgrounds. Intercultural couples can also experience problems if the values or belief systems they want to pass on to their children are at odds. This is a common issue for couples from different religious backgrounds, but it can also arise due to other cultural differences. For example, Jacob and Sarah wrestled with whether the children should be raised Jewish or Catholic. Jacob wanted his children to be raised in the Jewish religious and cultural traditions. Jacob also felt that his parents would be devastated if the children were not raised in the Jewish faith, especially given that they already disapproved of him marrying a non-Jew. In contrast, Sarah wanted their children to be raised Catholic and attend Catholic school like she did as a child. Like Jacob, she also felt that her family would disapprove if the children were not raised Catholic.

Gender Roles

Gender roles are another important area where cultural differences can potentially surface (Bustamante et al., 2011; Kellner, 2009; Maynigo, 2017; Singh et al., 2020). Men and women can be expected to take different roles and positions in society depending upon their cultural background. Some societies encourage men and women to adhere to more traditional gender roles, whereas others are less restrictive on the roles that men and women are expected to follow. In addition, some societies are more patriarchal, granting men more power than women, whereas other societies are more egalitarian. Conflict can arise for couples if they have very different expectations on the roles of men and women, as well as who has the power to make decisions in the relationships.

Positive Benefits

Although cultural differences can be a source of conflict for couples, it is equally important to note that they can be enriching (Blount & Young, 2015; Bustamante et al., 2011; Maynigo, 2017; Singh et al., 2020; Tili &

Barker, 2015). Many couples appreciate learning about another culture, which encourages them to be more open to other cultures. Some couples report that being with someone who is different has encouraged them to grow and change. For example, couples from different religious backgrounds frequently note that they grew spiritually by being with a partner from a different religious background, in part because their partner kept asking them why they believed or practiced what they did. These questions were often a catalyst for individuals to more closely examine their faith. Therefore, couples should try to find ways to celebrate rather than fear their differences.

Managing Cultural Differences

Couples can take various approaches to managing their cultural differences. Each of these approaches has implications for how a couple is balancing their individual identities with their identity as a couple. Depending upon the approach used, the couple may prioritize one or the other, or attempt to find a balance between both. Although the following examples focus on couples with religious differences due to my research in this area, the concepts also apply to couples who have other cultural differences (e.g., race/ethnicity).

Minimization

One approach some couples use to manage their differences is to minimize or ignore their individual differences (Killian, 2012). This allows the couple to avoid dealing with their cultural differences, and primarily focus on building the couple's identity. This was true of Noelle and Ryan early in their relationship. As noted earlier, Noelle was a devout Catholic, whereas Ryan questioned whether God existed at all. Initially, Ryan and Noelle focused on doing fun activities together when dating, avoiding serious conversations about their religious differences. Avoiding exploring cultural differences may work in the short term as the couple attempts to build a shared identity as a couple. However, it may present challenges in the long term, especially if it requires individuals to disown their cultural identity. As Ryan and Noelle fell more in love and began to talk about getting married, they realized that they would need to confront their religious differences, particularly if they had children. Therefore, the couple began to seriously explore their religious differences and what it meant in terms of the future of the relationship.

Coexisting

Other couples acknowledge their differences, but they choose to "agree to disagree." According to Seshadri and Knudson-Martin (2013), these couples retain their separate cultures, but do not attempt to integrate them into the relationship. They label these couples as coexisting. Coexisting couples appear to prioritize their individual identities over their couple identity with regard to cultural differences. As a result, they have a difficult time finding ways to connect in areas touched upon by their cultural differences. During their engagement, Ryan and Noelle discussed the role of God and religion in their lives. Although Noelle wished that Ryan would attend church with her, she accepted that he was not going to due to his serious questions about whether Got existed. Ryan respected that Noelle's faith was important to her, and even agreed to allow their children to be raised in the Catholic Church given how important this was to her. Once Ryan and Noelle got married, Noelle continued to attend the Catholic Church, while Ryan would stay home. The couple did not experience conflict over their religious differences, but the couple also did not find a way to create a shared identity or bond around religion.

Respectful Engagement

Another approach that couples can use is what I refer to as respectful engagement, which appears to be similar to what Seshadri and Knudson-Martin (2013) label as integrated couples. This approach balances a couple's individual and relational identities. Rather than minimize their differences, both parties engage in an active dialogue about their differences. Both partners make a concerted effort to learn more about each other's cultural background (Seshadri & Knudson-Martin, 2013). These couples focus on understanding how each person's cultural background has shaped them and why their cultural background is important to them. Learning about each other's cultural background conveys a strong love message: "I care enough about you that I want to learn what I can about you, including ways in which you may be different from me." Couples who practice respectful engagement seek to build a connection despite their cultural differences.

It is important for couples to explore each other's backgrounds to discover not only their differences, but also what they share in common (Bustamante et al., 2011; Seshadri & Knudson-Martin, 2013). In some cases, couples may discover commonalities that they did not realize existed either because they were not very knowledgeable or had misconceptions about the other person's cultural background. Often couples can find common ground if they examine the core beliefs or values that are behind specific beliefs or practices. Discovering shared core beliefs or values helps a couple build a shared couple identity despite their differences.

Demonstrating appreciation for their partner's culture is another important ingredient to respectful engagement (Seshadri & Knudson-Martin, 2013). Couples who successfully navigate cultural differences comment on how their partner is respectful of their cultural background rather than putting it down. Individuals can become defensive or even combative if they feel that their cultural beliefs, values, practices, or heritage are being put down. Therefore, individuals need to be careful about judging or belittling their partner's beliefs or practices. Taking the time to be curious about their partner's beliefs and practices can help suspend judgment and foster respect.

Katy and Sergio represent a couple who have practiced respectful engagement around religious differences in their relationship. When they began dating, Katy was active in the Lutheran church while Sergio was active in the Catholic church. Early on in their relationship, they began to talk about the meaning of religion in each of their lives because they knew spirituality was important to both of them. They also began to occasionally attend each other's worship services to learn more about the other's faith. Both individuals appreciated their partner's willingness to learn more about their own religious faith. Through their many talks, Katy and Sergio discovered that their fundamental beliefs about God were very similar, and that they also shared similar values on many issues. For Katy and Sergio, learning about their commonalities was helpful. After the couple married, both Katy and Sergio continued to remain active in their respective churches. At the same time, both frequently attended each other's church service as a way to stay connected spiritually. The couple also did volunteer activities as a couple in both churches. Thus, they were able to remain active in their separate churches, yet also nurture a shared spiritual bond as a couple.

Assimilation

A fourth approach that couples sometimes use to manage their cultural differences is for one partner to assimilate into the other's culture (Seshadri & Knudson-Martin, 2013). For example, one individual may convert to the other partner's religious faith. However, assimilation can occur in other areas as well, such as adopting cultural practices or beliefs consistent with the other person's culture. Assimilation can happen in one of two ways. In some cases, one individual chooses to adopt the other person's cultural beliefs or practices by choice. For example, Katy eventually decided after many years to change religious affiliation from Lutheran to Catholic. Through her exposure to the Catholic faith by virtue of her marriage to Sergio, she decided that the beliefs of the Catholic Church more closely aligned with her beliefs.

In contrast, some individuals feel pressured into adopting the other person's culture. Deidre was a practicing Catholic when she met Joshua, who was active in the Baptist church. Before Deidre and Joshua got engaged, Jason told Deidre that if they were to get married, it was important to him that the couple attend the same church for the unity of their family. Then he added, "But I will never be Catholic." Because Deidre wanted to marry Joshua, she left the Catholic Church to join Joshua's church. However, Deidre's resentment over being pressured to leave the Catholic Church resurfaced throughout the marriage. For example, when their first child was born, she was upset that she was not celebrating the baptism of her child with her extended family. Joshua acknowledged that pressuring her to change religious affiliation created problems in the relationship, and he later offered for her to return to the Catholic Church if she desired.

Therefore, it is important to assess why individuals have chosen to adopt the other person's cultural beliefs or practices. Like Katy, did the individual find something appealing and attractive in the other's culture that motivated them to change? Or, like Deidre, did the individual feel pressured in some way to adopt the other's cultural practices or beliefs? In some cases, individuals may not have a strong connection to their cultural identity, and they are therefore willing to adopt the other person's beliefs and practices for relationship harmony. When exploring assimilation, it is important to consider how power dynamics in the relationship may be influencing whose cultural practices or beliefs are being followed (Singh et al., 2020).

The Sociocultural Context in the Assessment of Couples

Couples are embedded within several larger systems, all of which have the potential to shape individuals and their relationships. It is important that the culturally sensitive therapist be able to place the couple within this larger context. Therapists must recognize how all of the cultural systems to which the individual belongs interact together to influence the individual. The term intersectionality is used to reflect the idea that multiple cultural forces can help define our experience or identity.

Knudson-Martin and Huenergardt (2010) have developed an approach called Socio-Emotional Relationship Therapy (SERT) that puts a socio-cultural perspective at the center of couple therapy. A key concept in SERT is sociocultural attunement, which requires that the therapist connect their understanding of both partners to the larger cultural systems that shape them. The goal of sociocultural attunement is for the therapist to develop an affective understanding of each client's experience and how it is informed by sociocultural factors.

The concept of sociocultural discourses is also important in the SERT approach and reflects the idea that members of a particular cultural group (e.g., gender, race/ethnicity, religion) have a shared way of thinking and talking about experiences. Different cultural contexts have different discourses, which shape how individuals view the world, themselves, and others. Messages internalized from various cultural contexts can influence how individuals think, feel, and behave in relationships. For example, Guillermo had a difficult time being vulnerable with his partner Rosalind, which impacted both their ability to resolve conflict and develop a more intimate relationship. Guillermo's difficulty with being vulnerable was rooted in messages he received about being a man from his family of origin ("big boys don't cry"), his Mexican heritage (machismo), and his time in the military as a Navy SEAL (warrior mentality). Recognizing the various sociocultural discourses that shape each partner is necessary to develop sociocultural attunement.

The SERT model is also attentive to the role of power in couple relationships. You should be asking yourself several questions regarding the couple to see if equality exists. First, do both partners have equal influence with each other? Examining how decisions have been made throughout the couple's history (Chapter 2) can inform your assessment of this. Second, are both partners able to be vulnerable with the other? For example, individuals in the more powerful position often may be more reluctant to be vulnerable to protect their position of power. Third, do both individuals take equal responsibility in terms of investing in the relationship? The partner in the less powerful position will often invest more in the relationship than the more powerful person. Fourth, are both individuals equally attuned to the needs of their partner? The less powerful person will generally be more attuned to the needs of the more powerful partner.

The following example illustrates how a sociocultural perspective, including an assessment of power, is helpful. In therapy, Andrea complained that she would like to see Nick help out more with cleaning the apartment and taking care of their 2-year-old daughter Whitney. Through assessment, the therapist discovered that the couple would get caught in a vicious cycle when addressing this issue. When Andrea would become frustrated with Nick, she would become critical of him, insisting that he change by contributing more to the housework and childcare. Nick, however, would resent how Andrea approached him when she asked for his help. He would feel like Andrea became his mother telling him to do his chores. Like a rebellious teenager, Nick would avoid doing what she asked to protect his sense of autonomy. However, this would only leave Andrea feeling unsupported and angry, leading to further anger and criticism.

The therapist also observed how gender socialization appeared to contribute to the couple's dynamics. The couple seemed to be following a traditional blueprint in terms of gender roles, which was explored with the couple. For example, the therapist asked where they had learned messages about gender roles, and how explicit the couple had been in agreeing to follow these roles. The therapist also noted that gender social-ization probably contributed to how each person felt in the dynamic (sociocultural attunement). For example, the therapist commented that many women felt a great deal of pressure living up to often unrealistic expectations of having a successful career and being the person primarily responsible for the household and childcare. Therefore, Andrea was likely feeling overwhelmed with the amount of responsibility in her life and would understandably desire help from Nick. The therapist also observed that Nick's strong need to protect his autonomy was probably tied to his gender socialization given that men often view the world from a hierar-chical perspective (Tannen, 2007). Nick resisted Andrea's demands to do more housework or childcare because he felt it put him in a one-down position, much like he felt as a child when his mother would reprimand him for not doing his chores.

However, the therapist was also attentive to how power was playing a role in the couple's dynamics. For example, Andrea is frustrated that she does not seem to have much influence over Nick's behavior when it comes to housework and childcare. Andrea is also dissatisfied that she is investing more in the relationship than Nick is. It also appears that Nick is more attuned to his own needs (protecting his time and autonomy) than to the needs of his wife or child. The therapist learns that Nick makes considerably more money than Andrea, which helps to create a power differential in the relationship. His position of greater power makes it possible for Nick to resist Andrea's desire that he contribute more to the relationship.

Culture and Acceptance From Others

Culture can also play a significant role in whether the couple experiences acceptance of their relationship (Blount & Young, 2015; Brunsma & Porow, 2017; Killian, 2001; Maynigo, 2017; Seshadri & Knudson-Martin, 2013; Silva et al., 2012). Intercultural couples, for example, may not be accepted by family members because the individual married someone outside the accepted group in terms of race/ethnicity or reli-gion. Likewise, interracial, minority, or same-sex couples can experience discrimination within their communities and society. Therefore, it is vital that therapists assess the extent to which the couple is accepted by others, as well as the impact this has upon the relationship.

Lack of acceptance by others can take many forms, including macroaggressions, microaggressions, and marginalization. Some couples experience macroaggressions, which are overt acts of aggression or discrimination against a couple due to race, sexual orientation, or other cultural factors. For example, some couples may experience housing discrimination due to their race/ethnicity or sexual orientation. Couples can also experience microaggressions, which are indirect or subtle actions against a marginalized group. For example, Jack and Nicholas would sometimes receive stares whenever they would walk in their community holding hands. The couple eventually moved to another area of the city that was more accepting of same-sex couples. Couples can also be marginalized due to cultural factors. Naomi and Justin, for example, were sometimes not invited to extended family events in Justin's family due to being an interracial couple.

Therefore, it is important to assess where the couple experiences acceptance and where they do not. Obviously, a lack of acceptance within one's extended family can have a significant impact on the couple. When Noelle and Ryan got engaged, Noelle's Catholic family expressed strong disapproval of the couple getting married because Ryan questioned whether God existed. The family even threatened not to attend the wedding. Noelle felt torn between her loyalty to her family and her love for Ryan. The stress over her family's lack of acceptance made Noelle question whether she should marry Ryan. You should also explore the extent to which friends support the couple's relationship. For example, Maxine's best friend questioned why Maxine, a White woman, would marry a Black man. Her friend cautioned Maxine that marriage is hard enough even without significant racial differences.

Assessing why family members or friends do not accept the relationship can sometimes reveal how to address the lack of acceptance. In some situations, lack of acceptance may be rooted in specific fears (Williams & Lawler, 2000). Noelle's family was not supportive of her engagement to Ryan because they feared Noelle would leave the Catholic Church and become distant from God if she married Ryan. Noelle reassured her parents that her Catholic faith was important to her, and that her marriage to Ryan would not change this. As Noelle continued to be active in her Catholic faith after getting married, her parent's fear diminished, and they became more accepting of her marriage to Ryan. Sometimes prejudice is the underlying cause of lack of acceptance. Offering education may be one way to reduce prejudice if it is rooted in misconceptions about a particular cultural group. Additionally, as family members or friends get to know the other partner over time, misconceptions and prejudices may be challenged and acceptance of the individual and the couple's relationship can grow (Seshadri & Knudson-Martin, 2013).

Finally, it is important to assess the effect that a lack of acceptance has upon the couple. A lack of acceptance can impact couples in at least two important ways. First, it can influence the level of social support that the couple has (Green & Mitchell, 2015; Leslie & Young, 2015). Many couples rely on their extended families for part of their social support. Therefore, you should assess if cultural factors influence the couple's level of support from their extended families. Are some family members supportive of the couple, while others are not? Is the couple cut off from one or both families? Do they remain involved with their families, but avoid talking about certain topics (e.g., religion) because it inevitably leads to conflict? For couples who struggle with a lack of acceptance by their families, friends may become the most important source of support. Therefore, you should assess the couple's social support outside of the family. In some cases, you may need to help the couple build up their social support network.

Second, a lack of acceptance can lead to minority stress (LeBlanc et al., 2015). Minority stress arises when individuals and couples from marginalized groups (e.g., minority couples, same-sex couples) experience added stress due to the prejudice and discrimination they experience. In addition to evaluating whether the couple is experiencing minority stress, you should also explore the impact that the minority stress is having upon the couple's relationship. In some cases, frustration from minority stress might be displaced into the relationship (Green & Mitchell, 2015). Different experiences around microaggressions can also contribute to problems for the couple (Leslie & Young, 2015). For example, individuals in interracial couples may experience different levels of microaggressions due to differences in racial privilege. Conflict can also emerge if individuals have different reactions to microaggressions. Charles and Yolanda, a Black couple in their late 50s, came to therapy to address conflict in their relationship. One source of conflict in the relationship that regularly occurred was when Charles would experience microaggressions during the day, and he would then come home to Yolanda to complain about the incidences. After Charles would describe the situations, Yolanda would not always agree with Charles's assessment that the incident was racially motivated, which could spark conflict for the couple. Although both Charles and Yolanda were Black and susceptible to experiencing microaggressions due to their race, Charles felt that he experienced more because he was a Black male.

Conclusion

This chapter has explored the important role that culture can play in relationships. For example, cultural differences between the partners have the potential to impact the couple in numerous ways. Table 5.1 lists important questions to consider when working with intercultural couples. When assessing the role of cultural differences in the relationship, be sure to consider not only the potential challenges these differences can pose for the couple, but also the ways in which the differences can enrich the relationship.

Table 5.1 Assessment Questions for Intercultural Couples

You are encouraged to consider the following questions when assessing the potential impact of cultural differences on an intercultural couple's relationship. It is important to remember that culture can be more broadly defined than just race or ethnicity.

1. What type of cultural differences (e.g., race/ethnicity, nationality, religion, socioeconomic status, level of acculturation) exist between the couple?

2. How do cultural differences impact the couple's communication (e.g., primary language spoken, expression of emotion)?

3. Are there differences in the importance and role of extended family due to differing cultural backgrounds (e.g., individualistic versus collectivist cultures)?

4. Are there any significant differences in values or core beliefs due to cultural differences?

5. How do cultural differences impact parenting?

6. Are there important differences in gender role expectations due to cultural differences?

7. What are the benefits that the couple experiences from their cultural differences?

In addition to looking at the impact of cultural differences on the couple's relationship, it is also important to assess how couples attempt to manage their cultural differences:

1. To what extent has the couple explored or discussed their cultural differences? Have they been receptive to exploring and learning about their cultural differences (e.g., respectful engagement), or have they attempted to minimize and avoid discussing their differences?

2. To what extent has the couple been able to find some commonalities in their cultural backgrounds (e.g., shared beliefs, shared values)?

3. Are the partners respectful of each other's differences, or do they criticize or negatively judge them?

4. To what extent has the couple been able to develop a shared connection around their cultural differences (e.g., respectful engagement versus coexisting)?

5. Has either partner assimilated to the other partner's culture? If so, what motivated the partner to do so (e.g., found the other culture attractive, felt pressure to do so, did not have a strong affiliation with their own cultural identity)?

As systems thinkers, we also need to be aware of the potential influence that sociocultural factors can have on all couples, not just intercultural couples. The combination or intersection of various cultural factors can shape how individuals create meaning and behave in their relationships. Cultural factors (e.g., gender socialization) can also influence power dynamics within a relationship. In addition, sociocultural factors can impact the level of acceptance that the couple experiences from family, friends, and others. Table 5.2 lists assessment questions that will encourage you to conduct your assessment with sociocultural factors in mind.

Table 5.2 Assessment from a Sociocultural Perspective

For all couples, you should consider how the sociocultural context influences each individual and their relationship. During assessment, it will be helpful to keep the following questions in mind:

1. How do sociocultural factors influence how the partners view themselves, their partner, or the relationship?

2. Is there a balance of power in the relationship (e.g., equal influence, equal willingness to be vulnerable, equal responsibility for the relationship, equal attunement to partner's needs)?

3. Do cultural factors impact the extent to which the couple's relationship is accepted by others (e.g., extended family, friends, community, society)?

4. If so, in what ways has the couple experienced a lack of acceptance from others (e.g., macroaggressions, microaggressions, marginalization)?

5. If the couple experiences a lack of acceptance from family and friends, what are the reasons behind it (e.g., fears, prejudices)?

6. What impact has a lack of acceptance had upon the couple (e.g., social support, experiencing minority stress)?

6

COMMITMENT

Commitment is the decision to remain together as a couple, even in the face of difficulties. Commitment is important for at least two reasons. First, it can help a couple survive the inevitable challenges that all intimate relationships face. All couples can experience ups and downs in the relationship, which can sometimes lead individuals to become dissatisfied with the relationship. A strong commitment can help couples weather these ups and downs, as well as motivate them to work on their relationship even during difficult times. Second, commitment creates a sense of safety in the relationship, which encourages individuals to show their true selves to one another. Individuals who feel uncertain about the future of a relationship may be reluctant to share the more vulnerable aspects of who they are. Thus, commitment is necessary for intimacy to grow in a relationship. This chapter will help you assess a couple's commitment, as well as factors that may weaken or strengthen their commitment.

DOI: 10.4324/9781003161967-6

How to Assess Commitment

There are a variety of ways in which you can assess an individual's level of commitment. One way is to simply ask individuals directly how committed they are to the relationship. Couples seeking help may have some ambivalence about the relationship, especially if they have been struggling with their issues for a significant length of time. Therefore, it is best to use a scaling question to assess each partner's level of commitment. For example, you might ask, "On a scale from 1 to 10, with 10 being extremely committed and 1 that you are ready to walk out the door, how would you rate your level of commitment?" Some therapists will follow up by asking why the score is not higher or lower than the answer provided by the individual. This can sometimes yield important insights into factors that support the individual's commitment or deter them from having a higher level of commitment.

As noted in Chapter 2, you can also use assessment instruments like the Marital Status Inventory (Weiss & Cerrato, 1980) or the Marital Instability Index (Edwards et al., 1987) to measure commitment. If you use the Dyadic Adjustment Scale (Spanier, 1976) to measure marital quality, responses to some of the questions can provide you with insight into each person's commitment. For example, Question 16 asks, "How often do you discuss or have you considered divorce, separation, or terminating your relationship?" Question 20 also asks individuals if they ever regret getting married or living together. Question 32 can also provide some insight into each individual's level of commitment based on what statement they endorse about the future of the relationship. Typically, commitment is strong for individuals who mark the top two choices because they are endorsing not only that the relationship is important to them, but they are very invested in seeing the relationship succeed (e.g., "I want very much for my relationship to succeed, and I will do all that I can to see that it does").

If one or both individuals are ambivalent about the relationship, then it will be important to determine what is behind their ambivalence. Does it reflect a loss of hope? Some individuals ideally want to see the relationship succeed, but they worry the relationship may not be salvageable. Individuals are typically reluctant to invest in something that they feel is potentially a lost cause. Fortunately, infusing hope will often lead to an increase in commitment to the relationship.

Some individuals threaten to leave a relationship or to divorce in the hope it will motivate their partner to enter therapy. These individuals are often invested in the relationship, but they feel the relationship will not succeed unless the partner is also willing to change. For these individuals, motivation to work on the relationship is not likely to be an issue, especially if their partner agrees to work on the relationship.

For other clients, their ambivalence may be significant enough to hinder their motivation to work on the relationship. For these individuals, both their hope and desire to see the relationship succeed have diminished. In these circumstances, it may be appropriate to consider discernment counseling (Doherty & Harris, 2017; Doherty et al., 2015), an approach that helps couples decide whether to divorce or separate, commit to working on the relationship, or maintain the status quo. Discernment counseling can be particularly helpful for couples where one person is invested in saving the relationship and the other partner is seriously contemplating ending the relationship.

Some individuals come to couple therapy having passed a point of no return in terms of their commitment to the relationship. One woman admitted she came to therapy knowing she wanted out of the relationship, but she hoped she would feel less guilty if she at least tried couple therapy. In some cases, individuals may not be aware that they have passed this point of no return. For example, Magdalena complained that her husband did not help around the house, and that she was tired of being his "servant" after 30 years of marriage. With the help of therapy, the husband's attitude began to change, and he started contributing to doing a lot more of the household chores. However, Magdalena continued to be unhappy despite the significant changes he was making. When this was explored further in therapy, Magdalena began to realize that no amount of change on her husband's part would remove the resentment that she had accumulated toward him over the years. Magdalena sought out a divorce shortly after this.

Factors That Can Impact Commitment

Commitment Issues Early in a Relationship

Imagine you see a couple at the altar getting married. What do you see? Why are they getting married? When we think about couples getting married, we typically envision individuals who are deeply in love. Although this is often the case, couples can get married for a variety of other reasons, which have the potential to impact whether they divorce or remain together. Therefore, it is important to explore how and why commitment developed for the couple through conducting a relationship history (see Chapter 2).

Eve is a 20-year-old woman who presents for therapy wanting to discuss her decision to leave her marriage to Mike. Eve describes growing up in a dysfunctional family. When she met Mike nearly 2 years ago, she was attracted to his "bad boy" image. He was a muscular 26-year-old mechanic who also rode in a motorcycle gang on the weekends. Her parents did not approve of her relationship with Mike, but they were also intimidated by him. When Mike asked Eve if she wanted to get married, she saw this as the opportunity to get out of her dysfunctional family. Although she admitted that she cared about Mike and he treated her well, she added that she never fell in love with him. Now she was highly ambivalent about the marriage, and she was seriously thinking of divorcing Mike after having been married less than a year.

Angelo and Erin have been dating for about 6 months. One day Erin unexpectedly discovers she is pregnant. When she tells Angelo about the pregnancy and her decision to have the baby, he decides the couple should get married. Although Angelo did not necessarily envision Erin as the one, he feels that marrying her is the honorable thing to do, especially given his strong Catholic upbringing. However, 3 years after getting married, the couple is in therapy due to chronic conflict in the relationship. Angelo is uncertain as to whether he wants to remain married.

In both of the above cases, factors in the couple's courtship have created commitment issues later in the relationship. It appears that Eve's decision to marry Mike was primarily driven by her desire to leave her family of origin. Now that she has successfully left her family, the primary motivation for the relationship appears to have disappeared, leaving her ambivalent about her marriage and questioning whether to remain. Therefore, it can be important to understand a person's motivation for getting married.

Likewise, Angelo felt pressure to get married because of the unplanned pregnancy. This had a lasting impact on him because he had this nagging question as to whether he would have married Erin had she not gotten pregnant. During therapy, Angelo decided to separate from Erin. After being separated for a month, Angelo realized that he loved Erin and returned to therapy to work on his marriage with Erin. The separation had the effect of resolving the commitment issue for Angelo because this time he had voluntarily chosen the relationship. Therefore, if you discover an unplanned pregnancy prior to marriage, you should explore whether or not the couple had considered marriage before learning of the pregnancy. If the couple had planned on marriage prior to the unplanned pregnancy, then commitment issues are not likely to arise. However, as the case of Angelo illustrates, commitment issues can arise if individuals did not entertained marriage at the time of the unplanned pregnancy.

Couples also need to be careful not to "slide" into marriage (Stanley et al., 2006), which can happen to couples like Jeff and Danielle. When they began dating, Jeff and Danielle quickly began seeing each other nearly every day. After dating for 3 months, Danielle's lease was about to expire, and she needed a new place to live. Because the couple was spending nearly every day together, they decided it would simply be easier if Danielle moved in with Jeff. This would allow both to save on expenses. The couple never discussed what this decision might mean for the future of the relationship. Six months later, the couple brought home a rescue dog that they decided to take care of together. They also pooled their money to buy new furniture and a large screen TV. These are just a few examples of how the couple's lives became more intertwined after living together. Up to this point, the couple never had a serious conversation as to where they saw the relationship going. After living together for 5 years, the couple decided that they might as well get married. Jeff and Danielle are an example of a couple that slid into marriage.

The danger for couples like Jeff and Danielle who live together out of convenience is that they may unexpectedly find that the costs associated with leaving a relationship start to increase. This can make it more difficult for the couple to end a relationship that they find is less than desirable. For example, if Jeff and Danielle split, who will get the dog? Some couples elect to stay in relationships and even get married because the costs of leaving a relationship are too high. However, some of these couples may eventually separate or divorce if they become dissatisfied enough with the relationship. Stanley et al. (2006) believe that this is one of the reasons why couples who cohabitate before marriage have a higher risk of divorce compared to those who do not. Their advice to couples is that they should "decide" rather than "slide" before living together or getting married.

Therefore, when examining the couple's history, you should consider how intentional the couple was in their decision to live together and get married. Was the decision to live together primarily driven by factors of convenience? Couples may be more vulnerable to sliding if their desire to live together is driven out of convenience. Did the couple discuss what living together meant in terms of their relationship status or future? For example, did the partners view living together as a sign of increased commitment or a step toward marriage? Once the couple began living together, what motivated them to get married?

Dedication and Constraints

The decision to stay in or leave a relationship is driven by both dedication and constraints. Dedication is an intrinsic desire to see the relationship continue. Dedication is often high early in relationships because individuals have a strong desire to see the relationship succeed due to the love that they have for one another. Constraints are factors that keep or restrain the individual from leaving a relationship. Thus, dedication reflects positive motivations to stay, whereas constraints reflect reasons not to leave.

Constraints to leaving a relationship can be either moral or pragmatic in nature. For example, a moral constraint might be viewing divorce as against one's religious beliefs or cultural norms. Other examples might include worrying how the children or partner will be impacted by a divorce, or a personal value that one always honors their commitments. Examples of pragmatic constraints include believing one will be unable to survive economically without the partner, losing shared property with a divorce, the fear of losing custody of the children, or believing there are no better alternatives that exist.

When Olivia came to therapy with her husband Edward, it was clear that both pragmatic and moral constraints were keeping her in her marriage. Olivia reported that she and Edward had grown distant over the years, eroding her sense of dedication to the marriage. However, Edward had recently been diagnosed with colon cancer. Olivia felt that she could not leave the marriage until Edward's health issues had been resolved. Otherwise, she would experience tremendous guilt. Olivia also admitted to being anxious about living on her own financially. She had grown accustomed to a comfortable lifestyle because Edward was a lawyer with a sizable income.

It is important to assess both dedication and constraints in a couple's relationship. Ideally, the couple will have a relationship that is characterized by high dedication, which will motivate them to work on the relationship in therapy. Unfortunately, as the case of Olivia illustrates, dedication can diminish or disappear over time for some couples. When this happens, individuals like Olivia can feel trapped in a relationship if constraints are high and dedication is low. The last section will explore protective factors that may help build or maintain dedication in a relationship.

Commitment Dilemmas

Assessment may also uncover dilemmas regarding commitment. Isabel and Gregory were one such example. Both Isabel and Gregory sensed the other person was holding back from fully committing to the relationship. As a result, each was fearful of fully committing to the relationship until they felt confident the other was truly committed. This naturally led to a stalemate that was not resolved until they each made a unilateral decision to invest in the relationship.

Individuals can also struggle with a commitment dilemma if they have suffered a major betrayal like an affair. Antoine was deeply hurt that his wife had an affair and questioned whether he should try to save his marriage. Antoine was reluctant to take the necessary emotional risks unless he felt confident the couple could successfully work through the affair. However, it was not possible for Antoine to know if they could heal from the affair unless he was willing to invest effort in working on the relationship. As his therapist noted, you don't know if you can climb a mountain until you try. Antoine's decision to invest in therapy to heal from the affair paid off. Although the process was a challenge, Antoine and his wife were able to successfully rebuild their marriage.

In both examples, resolving the dilemma required each partner to make a conscious decision to invest in the relationship even though the outcome was uncertain. Sometimes this decision is driven by an individual's values, such as wanting to honor their marriage vows. Others commit because of their belief that there is something in the other person or relationship that is worth taking the risk. Bernadette and Randy had worked through a brief affair that Randy had 2 years prior. The couple was now in therapy after a second infidelity by Randy. Understandably, Bernadette was highly ambivalent about continuing the relationship in light of a second infidelity. However, both agreed to explore through therapy the reasons why Randy had engaged in a second infidelity. One of the reasons that Bernadette was willing to give Randy another chance was that she had faith that Randy's core character was good despite the personal struggles that made him vulnerable to having two affairs. She was willing to remain in the relationship if he demonstrated a commitment to address these issues, which Randy did. Through some intensive individual and couple therapy, Randy made several significant changes in his life, including working through some childhood trauma that impacted his self-esteem and made him vulnerable to the past two affairs.

Protective Factors for Commitment

PREP offers a number of suggestions for how couples can strengthen their commitment to one another (Markman et al., 2010). These recommendations suggest a number of protective factors that can help couples maintain a strong commitment. Therefore, it can be helpful in your assessment to look for these protective factors. If these factors are absent, you can encourage couples to adopt these perspectives as a means of rebuilding or strengthening their commitment.

First, PREP emphasizes the need for couples to take a long-term perspective in terms of commitment to their relationship. If you follow the stock market, you will notice that stock prices go up and down over time. Some people invest when the market is good and leave when the market is down. However, this is a less effective strategy compared to regularly investing in the stock market. Despite some ups and downs, stocks trend upward if you take a long-term perspective. Thus, if you consistently invest in the stock market over time, you are likely to receive a positive return on your investment. In a similar manner, some individuals invest in a relationship when it is going well, but they do less when it is not going well. However, if individuals faithfully invest in their relationship despite the ups and downs that inevitably occur in relationships, then they will be rewarded for their continual investment.

Second, PREP encourages couples to focus on what they had in the beginning of the relationship. This will help couples remember why they fell in love and decided to devote their lives to one another. For distressed couples, doing a relationship history during the assessment (see Chapter 2) is one way you can help couples reconnect with these memories, which can renew their desire to work on the relationship. You can also explore what couples did during their courtship that they enjoyed. This is consistent with the PREP recommendation that couples be encouraged to do the things they did when they first fell in love. This can help rekindle the positive feelings that first brought the two of them together and led them to dedicate their lives to one another.

Third, PREP advises against individuals looking for or focusing on other alternatives. Individuals will sometimes think about what it might be like to be with someone else, especially if they are unhappy in their current relationship. In some cases, this may lead individuals to consider or engage in having an affair. If individuals adopt the "grass is always greener on the other side" attitude, then they will be more likely to look for or notice the flaws in their partner. Over time this will erode their satisfaction and commitment to their partner. Instead, it is best that they focus on what they like in their partner. Valuing their partner will help increase their dedication or commitment to them. As noted in Chapter 4, individuals will ideally develop a habit of noticing and expressing appreciation for their partner's positive qualities.

Fourth, explore the extent to which individuals focus on promoting the best interest of the relationship versus their own personal interests. PREP states that individuals will be more committed to the relationship if they feel that they are working together as a team, focusing on the "we" rather than the "me." Individuals who adopt a "me" perspective will selfishly focus on how the relationship meets their needs. In contrast, individuals who focus on the "we" perspective will be attentive to both their own needs and their partner's, striving to find win–win solutions for both.

Finally, another way for individuals to strengthen their commitment is to make their relationship a priority. It can be easy for couples to let other things take priority in their lives, like their children or their work. However, neglecting the relationship over time can lead to significant problems. Taking care of relationships is a lot like taking care of a car or truck. If individuals regularly invest in taking care of their vehicle, then they will be less likely to experience major problems or a breakdown. Couples who regularly invest time in taking care of their relationship will likewise experience fewer problems. The next chapter will discuss some of the ways in which individuals can invest in their relationship by showing caring behaviors toward their partner.

Conclusion

Commitment is an essential ingredient in maintaining a successful intimate relationship. It is the glue that holds the couple together, which is especially important when a couple goes through difficult times (as many couples do). You can use Table 6.1 to take an inventory of the commitment in a couple's relationship, identifying both strengths and areas of growth.

Table 6.1 An Inventory of Commitment

The following questions will help you take an inventory of how strong the commitment is in the couple's relationship:

1. How committed is each individual to the relationship?
2. If an individual is ambivalent or low in commitment, what accounts for this (e.g., loss of hope, threat to motivate partner)? To what extent will this ambivalence impact the individual's motivation to work on the relationship in therapy?
3. Are there any factors from the couple's relationship history that could be impacting commitment (e.g., unplanned pregnancy, sliding versus deciding)?
4. What is the level of dedication for each individual?
5. What are the moral or pragmatic constraints that keep individuals from leaving the relationship?

6. Are there any dilemmas around commitment (e.g., won't fully commitment unless the other commits)?

7. Does the couple take a long-term perspective with regard to their commitment, or is commitment tied to how they are feeling in the moment?

8. What did the two of them see in each other that made them want to commit to one another? Do they still see these things in each other? If not, how can they reconnect with them (e.g., do the things they did in their courtship)?

9. Do either of them look for better alternatives, thinking that the "grass might be greener on the other side"?

10. To what extent do they focus on the "we" rather than the "me" in the relationship? Is each person committed to the welfare of the other partner? Do they seek win-win solutions rather than just focusing on their own personal needs?

11. To what extent does each partner make their relationship a priority? Are there other things that take more of a priority (e.g., work, kids)?

7

CARING

Caring refers to behaviors we do to demonstrate our love and concern toward our partner. Showing our partner that we care acknowledges that they are valued and important in our eyes. Caring is critical to relationships because it addresses our need to be loved and valued as a human being. Individuals can tolerate a number of challenges or irritations in a relationship provided they are convinced that their partner loves or cares for them. However, conflict is likely to emerge if one or both partners begin to question whether their mate loves them.

Attending to caring in relationships is a lot like taking care of one's teeth. If you invest time and effort into caring for your teeth through brushing and flossing, then you will be more likely to have healthy teeth and gums. However, mild neglect may lead to a cavity, which can be easily remedied if it is identified and treated promptly. Unfortunately, further neglect can lead to more significant tooth decay. If allowed to go on too long, then the decay may become so severe that the tooth cannot be saved. This chapter will help you evaluate a couple's caring

DOI: 10.4324/9781003161967-7

to ensure that the relationship stays healthy and does not die from neglect.

Caring and Conflict

When working with couples, it is important to assess the extent to which both partners continue to show caring behaviors toward each other. For many couples who come to therapy, the amount of caring behaviors they do for one another has eroded over time. This erosion can happen for a couple of reasons.

First, the amount of time that some couples invest in showing caring behaviors can slowly erode due to other commitments in their lives. This is a common problem for couples with children. The time and energy required to take care of a household with children, along with work demands, can drain time and energy devoted to nurturing the relationship and each other.

Second, demonstrating caring behaviors can erode due to conflict. Continual conflict can lead individuals to distance from one another due to ongoing hurt feelings and as a way of avoiding conflict. Eventually, the problems in the relationship can seem bigger than the love and connection they share. Demoralization sets in, further undermining each person's investment in showing caring behaviors. Therefore, it is important to assess not only the amount of caring behaviors, but also the underlying reason why it has eroded if demonstrations of caring are infrequent.

Because caring can act as lubricant in the relationship, a reduction in caring behaviors can also increase friction and conflict in a relationship. This conflict, in turn, further reduces the motivation to show caring behaviors, thereby creating a vicious cycle. Reversing this downward spiral can be difficult, however encouraging couples to renew their efforts to demonstrate caring for each other can infuse hope into the relationship and remind them of the connection they once shared. Therefore, encouraging couples to increase caring behaviors can be an important step in helping couples rebuild their relationship (Baucom et al., 2015).

Different Forms of Caring: The 5 Love Languages

It is important to recognize that there are different ways of expressing caring. In *The 5 Love Languages: The Secret to Love That Lasts*, Chapman

(2010) describes five fundamental ways in which individuals can show that they care for their partner. Although there may be cultural variations on how these love languages are expressed, Chapman believes that the five languages described in this section are universal.

Words of affirmation as a love language is demonstrated through praising and complimenting one's partner. For example, Kevin loves it when Curtis compliments him on his cooking or comments on how handsome he looks. Individuals with words of affirmation as their love language want and expect to be told frequently by their partner, "I love you." Words of affirmation might also include offering encouragement or a vote of confidence before the partner faces a difficult challenge.

For individuals with *quality time* as their love language, they treasure having the undivided attention of their partner. Nasim feels loved by Aaron when he invites her to do shared interests together, like dancing, hiking, and sailing. Aaron and Nasim also protect one night a week for a date. Nasim looks forward to these nights when they go to different restaurants and enjoy conversations with one another.

For some individuals, receiving *gifts* is a tangible way of knowing they are loved. Gifts do not necessarily need to be expensive to be appreciated. Indeed, small gifts can be powerful if they are perceived as thoughtful. Tonya was touched when Ted brought home an inexpensive bouquet of her favorite flowers one day, even though there was no special occasion. Tonya loved Ted's gift for two reasons. First, the flowers showed that he had been thinking of her, which made her feel loved. Second, by giving Tonya her favorite flowers, Ted was showing that he had given special thought as to which flowers to get her. For those individuals with this love language, it really is the thought behind the gift that counts.

Acts of service as a love language is demonstrated through individuals doing things for their partner. Running an errand, doing a chore, or taking care of a task for one's partner can communicate that the individual is thinking of their partner's needs. Eric had a long day at work and was expected to do the dishes after dinner because Tracy had prepared the meal. However, Tracy recognized that Eric had a particularly difficult day. As a gesture of love, Tracy did the dishes that evening so that Eric could take extra time to relax. Eric appreciated Tracy's expression of caring through this act of service.

For some individuals, *physical touch* is their preferred love language. Holding hands, giving a hug, or reaching out to touch one's partner can mean the world to individuals with this love language. Christian loves it when Rachel surprises him by coming up from behind to give him a big hug. He also feels connected to Rachel when she gently strokes his arm or rests her hand on his lap when he is driving. Sexual intimacy can be another way in which individuals with this love language attempt to get their needs for touch met.

Individuals typically prefer to receive caring through one or two love languages. If individuals do not show their partner caring using their preferred love language, then their efforts to show love to their partner may go unrecognized. Elijah and Jessica struggled with this problem when they initially came to therapy. Elijah told the therapist that he was not sure if Jessica loved him. When asked why he felt this way, he replied that Jessica was not very verbally or physically affectionate. He continued by saying that in his family, people were very affectionate with one another and frequently told each other that they loved them. Jessica responded by saying that growing up in her family, individuals were not physically or verbally affectionate. However, she insisted that family members did love and care for one another. They showed this by doing things for one another. As a result, Jessica tried to show Elijah she loved him by doing things for him. Given that acts of service was Jessica's love language, it is not surprising that she expressed her desire that Elijah help out more around the house to show his caring, such as doing some laundry or giving the kids a bath in the evening. Elijah and Jessica clearly learned different love languages from their families growing up. Therefore, it is important that you help couples learn and speak each other's preferred love languages. You could encourage the couple to take the love language inventory at www.5lovelanguages.com/profile to learn each other's preferred love languages.

You also need to assess if individuals struggle to speak their partner's love language, especially if it is different from their own. Denzel, for example, learned that his wife Keneesha really liked words of affirmation as a love language. However, Denzel confessed that compliments from others had little meaning to him. To him, actions meant more than words. As a result, Denzel had a difficult time understanding why his words would mean so much to his wife. Therefore, he would frequently overlook opportunities to compliment or praise Keneesha. One day Denzel came up with the idea of putting a daily reminder in his phone to prompt him to offer some words of affirmation to Keneesha each day. This helped him become more consistent in offering words of affirmation to Keneesha, although he still missed opportunities to demonstrate his caring in this manner. Nonetheless, through practice, Denzel became more consistent and spontaneous in expressing through words his love for Keneesha. Although Keneesha would have ideally liked more words of affirmation, she recognized that this love language did not come naturally to Denzel and appreciated his efforts to become better at it.

Offering Support

Most individuals hope that their relationship will offer them refuge from the challenges or struggles they can encounter in life. Therefore, an important part of being in an intimate relationship is being able to offer support to one another. However, couples sometimes discover that they have difficulty offering the type of support that each person desires. Therefore, this can be an important area to assess with couples.

Gender differences between men and women can be one source of these difficulties because men and women traditionally offer support in different ways. Women often provide support by acknowledging that they understand what the other person is going through and validating their feelings. Tannen (2007) calls this the *gift of understanding*. For example, if Giselle calls her female friend to share an upsetting incident that she had with a coworker, her friend will likely validate how painful the incident was. Her friend may also offer a similar experience that she had to demonstrate she can appreciate why the incident was upsetting. Giselle feels closer to her friend because she has validated her experience and feelings. Tannen has observed that women often share their problems with one another as a means of forming a closer bond. Sharing one's troubles opens the door for intimacy, especially if the individual is vulnerable (see Chapter 3). Receiving validation in response to the disclosure strengthens the connection with the other person.

What happens when Giselle goes home and shares her experience with her partner Logan? If Logan behaves like most males, he will do one of two things when he hears Giselle's story. He may try to support

Giselle by trying to fix the problem, offering the *gift of advice* according to Tannen. For example, Logan could offer suggestions on how she might approach her coworker to fix the problem. Alternatively, Logan might try to reassure Giselle that everything will be fine, and not to worry about it.

Unfortunately, Logan's attempts to support Giselle are likely to leave her feeling invalidated. She is simply hoping that he will acknowledge how difficult the situation is for her. Instead, he offers unwelcome advice or minimizes her feelings telling her that everything will be fine. Rather than feeling closer to Logan, she is now upset by his efforts to "help" her.

It can also be important to assess how men feel when attempting to give support to their mates. In the previous example, Logan knows that he is trying to support Giselle, so he is both puzzled and irritated that his efforts to help are not being appreciated. Some men feel a lot of pressure to "fix" problems that their partners share with them. If the problem cannot be fixed, this can lead some men to feel like they are failing as mates. Some men may even withdraw to avoid these feelings of inadequacy, which further adds to the partner feeling unsupported. Sometimes men find it liberating to discover that simply listening can have a powerful impact on their partner.

In some cases, men can also be frustrated by the support they receive from women. If a man shares an incident that made him upset, he may feel invalidated if his partner says she knows exactly how he feels and offers an example where she had a similar experience. This may make him feel like the uniqueness of his experience is being discounted or invalidated.

When helping couples navigate this problem, encourage them to ask their partner what type of support they desire. For example, Logan might ask Giselle what he can do to support her. Would she like advice, or does she simply want him to listen and try to understand her feelings? In some cases, Giselle may want Logan's advice, but Logan will be wise to refrain from offering it unless he is sure that is what she wants.

It is also important to assess how much individuals confide in their partner about their concerns. Some individuals will share everything with their mate, whereas others will share very little. If one or both partners share little with one another, then it will be important to explore why. For example, Malcolm feared that his wife would view him as weak and insecure as a male if he shared his worries or concerns with her. Helping individuals overcome these barriers can strengthen the support and bond between the couple. In the Gottman approach (J. S. Gottman & J. M. Gottman, 2015), couples are encouraged to have a "Stress-reducing Conversation" where they take 20 minutes each day to share with one another stresses they are experiencing outside the relationship. During the conversation, partners focus on being empathic listeners rather than attempting to problem-solve.

Building and Maintaining Connection

Bids for Emotional Connection

Couples seek to build and maintain connection through small, daily gestures called bids for emotional connection (J. M. Gottman & J. S. Gottman, 2015). When individuals make these gestures, they are expecting their partner to respond in a positive manner, such as demonstrating interest in what they are saying, asking questions, having a conversation, showing empathy, or offering assistance and support. However, individuals can respond negatively by ignoring the bid for connection (turn away) or being impatient or upset with the bid (turn against). For example, Brooke would seek connection from her partner when he came home from work by making statements like, "The baby was fussy today." Hector would remain silent, thinking that this was a statement of fact rather than a question, and therefore it did not require a reply. What he did not recognize was that this was a bid for emotional connection rather than simply sharing information. By remaining silent, Hector was turning away from Brooke's bid for emotional connection. Instead, the therapist encouraged Hector to respond in a positive manner. For example, Hector could express interest in what Brooke was saying by asking questions, such as asking why she thought the baby was fussy. Or Hector could express empathy, stating, "That must have made for a difficult day for you." Perhaps even better, Hector might ask, "Do you need me to take care of the baby for an hour, so you have some time alone to recharge your batteries?" Each of these responses could help Brooke feel connected to Hector.

It is important that you assess the extent to which couples are able to positively respond to each other's bids for emotional connection.

A dissertation study by Janice Driver (2006, as cited by J. M. Gottman & J. S. Gottman, 2015) found that newlywed couples that divorced after 6 years positively responded to only 33% of their partner's bids, whereas the couples who stayed married positively responded to 86% of their partner's bids. Do individuals recognize when their partner is making a bid for connection? Do they positively respond to the bid for connection, or do they turn away from or turn against them?

Each person's meta-emotion style is an important factor that can influence how individuals respond to their partner's bids for emotional connection (J. M. Gottman & J. S. Gottman, 2015). Meta-emotions are our emotions about emotions. John Gottman's research has identified two overall types of meta-emotions: emotion-dismissing and emotion-coaching. Another meta-emotional type called emotion-out-of-control exists, which is a subcategory of emotion-dismissing. Individuals who are emotion-dismissing tend to ignore or dismiss the importance of emotions. As a result, they typically have a limited vocabulary about emotions. They prefer to take action rather than be introspective about their emotional experience and what it might mean. Instead, they will compartmentalize their emotions to avoid focusing on them. Individuals who are emotion-dismissing can also be dismissive of emotions in others. Therefore, they can become impatient or critical of other people's emotions, particularly their negative emotions. For example, they might tell a depressed person to "pull themselves up by the bootstraps" and get over it. Due to gender socialization, men are more likely to be emotion-dismissing than women.

As noted, a subcategory of emotion-dismissing is emotion-out-of-control. Although both dismiss the value of understanding emotions, emotion-out-of-control individuals have difficulty compartmentalizing their emotions compared to other emotion-dismissing individuals. As a result, they can sometimes feel overwhelmed by their emotions, especially negative emotions like anger. Consistent with this, they often associate negative emotions with dangerous adjectives, such as explosive anger.

In contrast to emotion-dismissing individuals, those who are emotion-coaching value emotions because of the information they can provide them. Just as the military collects intelligence information to learn about what is going on in the world and assess when possible action might be required, emotions do the same in our personal lives. Because emotion-coaching individuals value what emotions can reveal, they tend to have a richer emotional vocabulary than those with an emotion-dismissing approach. They will also spend more time reflecting upon and trying to understand what their emotions mean.

When working with couples, you should assess the meta-emotion style for each partner and note if there is a mismatch. A meta-emotion mismatch is a risk factor for divorce (J. M. Gottman & J. S. Gottman, 2015). This is understandable if you think of the different ways an emotion-dismissing person might respond to a bid for emotional connection, especially if the bid is tied to negative affect in some way. In the example of Hector and Brooke, the therapist discovered that the two individuals had different meta-emotions. Brooke was emotion-coaching, while Hector was emotion-dismissing. When Brooke complained about the baby being fussy, she hoped and assumed that Hector would be empathetic to the difficult day that she had with the baby. However, because Hector was emotion-dismissing, he did not focus on the emotional implications behind Brooke's statement. Furthermore, if he did respond, it was often to give advice on how to better take care of the baby rather than empathize with the challenges of having a fussy baby. In some cases, emotion-dismissing individuals will even be critical of the other's negative emotions or complaints, which the Gottman approach refers to as turning against (rather than turning away from) an emotional bid.

The Gottman approach addresses meta-emotion mismatches using a variety of interventions (J. M. Gottman & J. S. Gottman, 2015). For example, you can teach individuals (especially the emotion–dismissing partner) to develop greater awareness and language around their emotions. Both partners are encouraged to make their needs or bids for emotional connection explicit with their partner. For example, Brooke can tell Hector, "I missed seeing you today while you were at work. Can I tell you a little bit about my day so we can reconnect?" Also, similar to what Hector's therapist asked him to do, individuals are encouraged to ask open-ended questions and make statements that express interest and empathy.

Mutually Rewarding Activities

Another important element of caring that should be assessed is the extent to which couples do mutually rewarding activities together. For most couples in American society, developing an intimate relationship begins through dating. Dates typically center around activities where couples get opportunities to talk and get to know each other. As the couple develops a closer bond, they naturally want to spend more time together enjoying each other's company. Spending time with each other, in turn, strengthens the couple's connection with each other.

However, a couple's need to spend quality time together does not end once the two become a committed couple. If a couple is to remain successful in their relationship, they will need to continue to find ways to nurture their relationship through spending quality time together. There is certainly some truth to the saying, "Couples who play together, stay together." Therefore, it is important to assess if the couple spends quality time together nurturing their relationship and enjoying each other's company.

Couples with children may find it more difficult to spend protected time together as a couple (see Chapter 11). Raising children requires a huge investment in time, as well as emotional and physical energy. Time that used to be devoted to nurturing the relationship can now be consumed with taking care of children and their needs. The wise couple continues to set aside time for the relationship, such as having regular date nights without the children. Otherwise, couples may find that the quality of their relationship erodes over time if they do not protect time to nurture it.

If a couple is not spending a sufficient amount of time together, it is important to explore and address the reasons why. Does the couple see the value in protecting time together as a couple? Does the couple complain of challenges they will face if they try to institute a regular date night? Many couples will state money or childcare as concerns. For example, it may cost money to do some activities (e.g., go to a movie or dinner) or to hire a babysitter. These couples need to be resourceful and creative to overcome these barriers. For example, some couples exchange babysitting nights with another couple or rely on extended family for babysitting. Couples can also find activities that may be free or require little money to do, such as doing hikes, going to the beach, window-shopping, or free public events. Some couples may need to prioritize dates as a necessary expense like medical insurance to protect the long-term health of their relationship.

Another potential threat to couples spending time together is conflict. Couples who are fighting may spend less time together to avoid conflict. When this happens, the relationship becomes more vulnerable because the fighting not only pulls the couple apart, but there is not the counterbalancing force of doing pleasurable things together to offer positive reinforcement for the relationship. Once this process begins, the couple will find that simply reducing or eliminating conflict does not automatically restore a sense of connection. Couples will need to make independent efforts to restore their connection by doing pleasurable activities together.

Sometimes couples will state that they don't know what activities they want to do together. For these couples, it may be helpful to ask what activities they did when dating. Couples rebuilding their relationship may benefit from doing the very things they did to build a connection in the first place. For example, Raymond and Clarissa initially met through a support group meeting, and then began to spend time with one another outside these meetings by going to the beach or flying kites. The two began to spend more and more time together, eventually deciding to move in together after Raymond's lease ended. Unfortunately, the couple stopped doing the activities they had previously enjoyed doing after moving in together. Conflict also began to emerge for the couple over issues of responsibility and control. Increasing conflict in the relationship led the couple to seek out therapy. One important intervention for the couple was to resume doing pleasurable activities they enjoyed early in the relationship, such as going to the beach and flying kites. This infused a sense of hope and energy in the relationship, which made it easier to deal with the other issues around responsibility and control. Doing these fun activities together not only helped the couple reconnect, but it also reminded them why they fell in love with each other in the first place.

In addition to assessing the amount of time the couple spends together, you should assess its quality. This is illustrated by Robert and Carolyn's story. Robert recently retired, resulting in the couple spending considerable time together at home. Ironically, this increase in time together actually created conflict for the couple, in part because Carolyn felt like she no longer had any personal space now that Robert was home all the time. Furthermore, the couple was not actually doing rewarding activities together as a couple when they were at home. The therapist's solution was to encourage Robert to find some volunteer work that he found meaningful and would get him out of the house. In addition, the couple was encouraged to spend time together doing activities or dates that they both found mutually fun to do. The combination of reducing the amount of time together and improving its quality proved to be very beneficial to the couple.

An important way to improve the quality of time together is to actively seek out new and exciting experiences (Aron et al., 2000; Malouff et al., 2015). Always doing the same things can lead boredom to set in, making the time together less rewarding. Therefore, it is helpful to assess if couples regularly incorporate new or novel experiences into their relationship. Traveling together is often one way that couples do this, but it can also be accomplished in other ways, such as trying new activities together, eating at new restaurants, or visiting new places locally.

Rituals

Another way that couples can stay connected is through rituals (J. M. Gottman & J. S. Gottman, 2015; J. S. Gottman & J. M. Gottman, 2015). These rituals can be formal or informal. For example, couples often have rituals on how they will celebrate important holidays or events like birthdays or anniversaries. Couples may also have rituals in their daily lives that maintain connection, such as eating meals together or offering each other a kiss when reuniting after being away from each other. Rituals can also exist around how to spend vacations, what to do when one partner becomes ill, or how to initiate sex. Therefore, when assessing a couple's level of connection, it may be important to explore what rituals the couple have woven into their relationship.

Conclusion

Caring reflects the variety of ways in which couples share their love and develop a connection with one another. Caring is multidimensional, requiring assessment in several domains to fully capture its complexity (see Table 7.1). One element of assessing caring is examining each person's love language, including each individual's ability to speak their partner's preferred love language. It is also important to assess how each partner tries to offer support (e.g., gift of understanding, gift of advice), and whether it meets the partner's needs. Caring also encompasses the various ways that couples maintain connection to one another, including responding to each other's bids for emotional connection, doing mutually rewarding activities together, and creating rituals. Sexual intimacy is another important element of caring, which will be explored in the next chapter.

Table 7.1 Assessing Caring Behaviors

The following questions can assist you in assessing caring in a couple's relationship:

1. To what extent does the couple show caring behaviors toward each other? If low, what factors (e.g., conflict, other demands) have led to the erosion of caring behaviors?

2. What are the preferred love languages for each partner?

3. To what extent do individuals know and speak each other's love language? What are potential barriers, if any, to each partner speaking the other's love language(s)?

4. How do individuals typically offer support to each other? Is it typically through offering the gift of advice or the gift of understanding?

5. How much do individuals seek support or confide in each other?

6. Do individuals recognize their partner's bids for connection? To what extent do individuals positively respond to their partner's bids for emotional connection?

7. What is the meta-emotion style for each partner? To what extent do meta-emotions impact each partner's ability to respond to bids for emotional connection or offer emotional support?

8. How often does the couple do pleasurable activities together (e.g., dates)? If infrequent, what are the barriers (e.g., time, money, childcare) to doing more?

9. What kind of pleasurable activities does the couple enjoy doing? What kind of new activities or experiences would they be interested in doing?

8

ASSESSING A COUPLE'S SEXUAL RELATIONSHIP

In the previous chapter, the importance of assessing caring behaviors was addressed. One important way that couples can express caring is through sex. For most couples, sex is a way of expressing love and developing a closer bond with one another. Therefore, establishing a satisfying sexual relationship is important to building a successful relationship. Unfortunately, problems can emerge for couples in their sexual relationship, which robs them of an important source of enjoyment and connection. McCarthy and McCarthy (2014) believe that a positive sex life contributes 15–20% to couples having a satisfying relationship, whereas a negative sex life diminishes a couple's satisfaction by 50–70%. Therefore, it is important to assess the quality of a couple's sexual relationship and address any problems that exist.

This chapter will begin by offering some general principles to guide you in assessing sexual problems in a relationship. This will be followed by a discussion of factors that commonly create problems in sexual functioning. Factors unique to various disorders will be examined in the

DOI: 10.4324/9781003161967-8

subsequent section. In addition to assessing for sexual problems, it is also important to assess for factors that help promote or protect a healthy couple's sexual relationship. Therefore, a section is devoted to assessing these factors as well. Finally, the chapter concludes with how to do an assessment around pornography, which couples may report as a presenting issue.

General Principles

When assessing a couple's sexual relationship, the following principles or guidelines can help make your assessment more effective.

Ask all couples about their sexual relationship – For many couples, asking about their sexual relationship will create anxiety due to the private nature of sex. However, it is important that you ask about a couple's sexual relationship because many couples will be experiencing problems in this area, even if they don't volunteer this information.

Assess your own comfort level talking about sex – Couples may not be the only individuals in the therapy room uncomfortable talking about sex. Sometimes therapists have their own anxiety or discomfort talking about sex, which can lead to avoiding asking about sex. Therefore, you should assess your own comfort level talking about sex so you don't avoid inquiring about a couple's sexual relationship (Buehler, 2017). Part of your assessment should also include your comfort in asking specific questions about sex or sexual practices. For example, a thorough assessment may require asking clients about their masturbation practices, which may be a more threatening topic to address than asking about the overall quality of a couple's sexual relationship. If you are uncomfortable talking about sex, what is the source of that discomfort? What messages did you learn about sex growing up? How knowledgeable do you feel about sexual issues? Typically, therapists become more comfortable talking about sex as they become more knowledgeable.

Conduct the assessment using a biopsychosocial perspective – Sexual disorders can be challenging to assess and treat because they may involve multiple domains, including biological, psychological, and relational factors. For example, a man may begin to have difficulty getting full erections due to early signs of cardiovascular disease (biological). If the man begins to develop performance anxiety about his erections (psychological), then he will experience even more problems obtaining an erection. If the man's partner also becomes critical of his erectile difficulties (relational), then this will add to his performance anxiety and further inhibit his ability to get an erection. Therefore, it is key that assessment of sexual problems be done from a biopsychosocial perspective to ensure all relevant factors have been considered.

Determine if the sexual disorder is primary or secondary, as well as generalizable or situational – When assessing sexual disorders, it is important that you consider two important questions. First, is the sexual disorder primary or secondary? A sexual problem is primary if it has always existed. For example, a woman who has never experienced an orgasm would be classified as having primary anorgasmia. In contrast, if she was previously able to have orgasms but now experiences problems, then she would have secondary (sometimes called acquired) anorgasmia.

Second, is the sexual disorder generalizable or situational? If the disorder is generalizable, the individual always experiences the problem. However, if the individual only experiences the problem in certain contexts, then it is situational. An individual who has lost all interest in any sexual activity would be classified as generalizable. However, if the individual has lost sexual desire with their partner but still has sexual desire in other ways (e.g., desire for someone else, masturbation), then it would be classified as situational.

Combining the answers to these two questions often provides important clues as to whether the sexual disorder has a biological or psychosocial cause. Sexual disorders that are secondary (acquired) and situational are typically due to psychosocial causes. In contrast, disorders that are secondary and generalizable are likely due to biological causes. Assessment is more challenging if the sexual disorder is primary and generalizable. Biological factors should definitely be ruled out, but psychosocial causes are still possible (e.g., childhood sexual trauma).

Evaluate for co-occurring sexual disorders – It is not uncommon for one sexual disorder to co-exist with another. For example, a man who has difficulty getting erections may eventually develop a low desire for sex to avoid his erectile difficulties. Likewise, a woman who experiences sex as painful (dyspareunia) may develop low desire or difficulties achieving an orgasm.

It is also important to evaluate the possibility of a co-occurring disorder existing with the partner. Manuel recently began to experience difficulties getting erections during intercourse with his partner Audrey. Manuel reports no difficulties getting erections during masturbation. Given that Manuel's erectile difficulties are secondary (acquired) and situational, the therapist suspects a psychosocial cause. Further assessment reveals that Audrey has recently entered menopause. As a result, she now experiences pain during intercourse. Whenever the couple attempts to have sex, Audrey becomes anxious because she anticipates that penetration will be painful. Manuel loses his arousal when he senses that Audrey is becoming anxious rather than aroused during foreplay. His lack of arousal in response to Audrey's fears of sexual pain leads to his difficulty getting erections.

Common Causes of Sexual Disorders

Medical Issues

When assessing for possible causes of sexual problems, it will be important that you rule out biological causes, especially if the sexual disorder is acquired and generalizable. Several diseases have been commonly linked to sexual disorders. For example, diabetes can impact desire, arousal (e.g., erections), and the ability to orgasm. Erectile difficulties can also be an early indicator of cardiovascular disease for men (Kalogeropoulus & Larouche, 2020). Neurological diseases (e.g., multiple sclerosis) or nerve damage from injuries and surgeries can also impact sexual functioning. Hormone levels are also linked to sexual functioning. For example, extremely low testosterone levels can reduce sexual desire, as well as other hormones (e.g., hypothyroidism, high prolactin levels). If biological factors are a suspected cause, a referral for a medical evaluation is warranted.

Mental Health Issues

Mental health disorders should be ruled out as a possible cause of sexual difficulties (Buehler, 2017). For example, depression is often linked with low sexual desire, as well as other sexual problems. Anxiety and PTSD can also reduce an individual's sexual desire or arousal. Some women report that ADHD can lead them to being distracted during sex, which can interfere with their ability to become aroused and to orgasm. There-fore, you should be vigilant as to the possible role that mental health issues may be having upon an individual's sexual functioning.

Medications

Medications also need to be ruled out as possible causes of sexual dis-orders (Buehler, 2017). For example, SSRI antidepressants have been known to reduce sexual desire in many individuals or delay ejaculation in men. Other medications such as antipsychotics, anti-seizure medications, high blood pressure medications, opioids, and birth control pills can also create sexual difficulties. Therefore, it is important to determine if the onset of a sexual disorder corresponds to any changes in medication.

Substance Use

Substance use should also be ruled out as a cause of sexual difficulties (Buehler, 2017). For example, acute and chronic alcohol use can neg-atively interfere with sexual functioning (e.g., ability to get erections). Other drugs such as cocaine and heroin can also impact sexual func-tioning (e.g., cocaine users may experience delayed ejaculation). Even substances such as nicotine have been known to reduce sexual desire in some people. Eliminating or reducing substance use may be required to address the sexual disorder.

Performance Anxiety

Individuals can begin to worry about their sexual performance, which is often referred to as performance anxiety. Performance anxiety can cause a sexual disorder, or it can arise due to a pre-existing sexual disorder. For example, a man may begin to develop performance anxiety due to pre-mature ejaculation. His anxiety about ejaculating prematurely may lead to a reduction in arousal, which interferes with his ability to obtain or maintain erections. A partner's response to the sexual problem can also create or intensify the individual's performance anxiety. For example, Anton was upset that Melinda did not have orgasms during sex with him. Anton viewed Melinda's inability to have an orgasm as a sign that he was not a good lover. As a result, Melinda began to feel pressure to have an orgasm to please her partner. Unfortunately, her anxiety about having an orgasm made it difficult for Melinda to relax and enjoy sex, making it impossible for her to have an orgasm during sex with Anton.

Sensate focus is a technique that sex therapists often use to help couples bypass performance anxiety (Buehler, 2017). During sensate focus, individuals take turns touching their partner in a sensual way that is pleasing to them. In sensate focus I, couples avoid touching each other's genitalia or the woman's breasts. In sensate focus II, the genitalia and woman's breasts can be touched. Sexual intercourse is prohibited when couples engage in sensate focus I or sensate focus II exercises. Sensate focus can help reduce performance anxiety by helping individuals direct their focus to sensual pleasuring rather than having an orgasm. However, sensate focus is also a valuable assessment tool. How the couple responds to the sensate focus exercises can provide important information, such as uncovering negative beliefs about sex or inhibitions (see the next section).

Negative or Unrealistic Beliefs About Sex

Negative beliefs about sex can interfere with sexual functioning. Therefore, it is important to assess if individuals have healthy and positive beliefs about sex. For example, do individuals feel they deserve sexual pleasure? Unfortunately, some women internalize the message that sex should focus on the man's pleasure rather than her own pleasure. Likewise, some men focus so much on their performance that it comes at the expense of their own sexual pleasure. If individuals see sex as shameful, then this will negatively impact their sexual functioning. As a young child, Tatum was caught by his father "playing doctor" with a neighborhood girl. The father punished his son using extreme physical abuse, which led to Tatum developing a sense of shame regarding sex. This contributed to his low sexual desire in adulthood, especially with intimate partners.

Individuals also need to have realistic expectations about sex to avoid being disappointed or anxious about their sexuality. If a man has unrealistic expectations about how long he should last during sex before ejaculating, he may develop a sense of inadequacy or anxiety about his performance even though he may be normal for a man. Having realistic expectations also means understanding that everyone will have the occasional unfulfilling experience during sex with their partner. McCarthy and McCarthy (2014, p. 9) state that it is not uncommon for one partner to have a more fulfilling experience than the other, although both may enjoy the experience. They also note that 5–15% of a couple's sexual experiences will be "mediocre, unsatisfying, or dysfunctional." Couples should not be alarmed when this happens, but they should take these experiences in stride.

It is important to assess if unrealistic expectations may be underlying a sexual difficulty. For example, Everett would initially get an erection during foreplay. However, he would sometimes lose his erections with extended foreplay. When this happened, Everett told himself that he would not be able to get his erection back and that sex was over before it even had begun. Everett's therapist normalized that men could lose their erections during extended foreplay, yet assured him that he could regain his erection with additional stimulation during foreplay. To reinforce this, the therapist had Everett practice the wax and wane technique with his partner. During foreplay, Everett was instructed to deliberately lose his erection. His partner was then instructed to provide manual or oral stimulation to help Everett regain his erection. The couple was asked to repeat this process twice. Through normalization and the wax and wane technique, Everett regained his confidence in his sexual performance.

When challenging problematic beliefs about sex, it can be helpful to determine where the beliefs were learned. Sometimes family of origin messages about sexuality or religious socialization can create negative messages about sex. Societal messages about sex can also lead to negative beliefs or unrealistic expectations about sex that are harmful to a healthy view of sex. For example, movies typically depict two people having intense and passionate sex. For most couples though, the intensity of sexual passion that they experience in the beginning of the relationship diminishes with time (McCarthy & McCarthy, 2014). Some couples in long-term relationships can become disappointed if sex does not compare to the sex they had in the beginning of the relationship or what they see depicted in the movies. Pornography can also contribute to individuals having unrealistic expectations about sex, such as the size of various body parts or the types of sexual behaviors that individuals enjoy (Maltz & Maltz, 2010).

Trauma

Trauma can also interfere with sexual functioning, especially if the trauma is related to sexual assault or sexual abuse (Buehler, 2017; MacIntosh et al., 2020). Negative associations between the present and past trauma can impact an individual's ability to have a positive experience around sex. For example, Dhalia was sexually abused as a child by a man who had facial hair and was sweaty. Therefore, Dhalia would sometimes experience painful memories of her past abuser if her husband was not clean-shaven and freshly showered when he approached her for sex. This would lead her to turn down her partner's advances for sex.

Sexual Inhibitions

Negative beliefs about sex or negative sexual experiences can create sexual inhibitions that interfere with sexual functioning. Therefore, you should assess for the possible presence of sexual inhibitions. Sexual inhibitions can take many forms, including inhibitions about being naked, making sexual requests, or having an orgasm. McCarthy and McCarthy (2014) recommend that individuals who have inhibitions follow four steps to overcome them. The first step is for the individual to acknowledge to their partner and themselves that they have an inhibition. The second step is to decide whether the inhibition can be overcome, modified, or worked around. Third, work is done to change the inhibition, which typically requires some form of systematic desensitization and challenging negative thoughts or attitudes associated with the inhibition. In the fourth step, individuals must maintain their gains by continually confronting their inhibition rather than avoiding it.

Sexual Preferences and Sexual Orientation

In some cases, sexual preferences can create sexual problems, especially if there is a mismatch between what an individual desires and reality. For example, an individual who wishes to incorporate certain fetishes or sexual practices into sex may have difficulty with arousal and becoming orgasmic if the partner is unwilling to follow the mate's sexual preferences. Issues around sexual orientation can also create problems. Peter and Hallie struggled with their sexual relationship throughout the course of the marriage, largely due to Peter's low sexual desire. After being married for six years, Peter admitted to Hallie that he was primarily attracted to men rather than women.

Relationship Issues

It is important to rule out relational problems as a possible cause of sexual difficulties. For example, individuals may be angry with their partner for how they are being treated in the relationship. This anger may reduce their desire to have sex with their partner or reduce their ability to enjoy sex with the partner. A lack of closeness or emotional intimacy in the relationship may be another underlying cause of sexual problems. Juliana and Simon grew increasingly distant in their marriage. When Simon would occasionally approach Juliana for sex, she felt that it was not so much a bid for closeness but simply a way to obtain sexual gratification. Therefore, Juliana would typically turn down his advances because she did not feel emotionally connected to him.

Even if relationship factors are not the original cause of the sexual problem, relationship issues may still need to be assessed and addressed in therapy. For example, a partner's critical response to a mate's sexual disorder may create or reinforce the performance anxiety, exacerbating the problem. In addition, a couple may be hesitant to resume having sexual relations after a long abstinence due to an untreated sexual problem.

Specific Considerations for Various Sexual Disorders

Low Sexual Desire

A common problem that can arise between couples is where one person has a lower desire for sex than the other. In some cases, both partner's levels of desire may be in the normal range, with one person's desire on the higher end of the normal range and the other's on the lower end of the normal range. For many couples, however, one individual may have little or no desire for sex.

Partners may not only differ in their levels of desire, but also in the type of desire they predominantly experience. Sexual desire can be either spontaneous or responsive (Brotto & Velten, 2020; Dürr, 2009).

Individuals with spontaneous desire will have thoughts about sex, and thus seek out opportunities to have it. Marcus often thinks about having sex with his wife Emily, and he is typically the one to initiate sex with her. In contrast, individuals with responsive desire will often not think much about sex unless they are approached for sex. If the conditions are right, the individual will accept or be responsive to their partner's request to have sex. For example, Emily is typical of a person with responsive desire. She does not often think about sex; however, she enjoys sex with Marcus when they do have sex. If Emily feels emotionally connected to Marcus, then she will typically be responsive to his request to have sex. Although she may not feel sexually aroused at that moment, she may accept his invitation to have sex to please him or strengthen the connection between the two of them. Conversely, if the conditions are not right (e.g., fatigue, stress, conflict in the relationship, feeling disconnected), then Emily will not be responsive to Marcus when he approaches her for sex.

Unlike individuals with spontaneous desire, individuals with responsive desire develop arousal and desire for sex at the same time rather than desire preceding arousal. As Emily becomes more aroused through foreplay, her desire for sex builds. Her increasing desire also makes it easier for her to become further aroused, eventually leading to an orgasm.

Individuals can have both spontaneous and responsive desire. Spontaneous desire is typically more common among men than women, although many women also experience spontaneous desire. In contrast, many women would characterize their primary type of desire as being responsive rather than spontaneous.

You should assess if differences around spontaneous and responsive desire are impacting how a couple relate around sex. In heterosexual relationships, the man is often the primary initiator of sex due to his spontaneous desire for sex. (Be aware that there are exceptions to this. In some relationships, the woman may have a higher spontaneous desire than the man.) Men also use sex as a vehicle for achieving closeness with their mate. Sex makes many men feel emotionally connected to their partner in an intimate relationship. In contrast, women often see emotional connection as a prerequisite to having sex due to their responsive desire. Thus, men who are not attentive to their partner's needs outside the bedroom may find that their partner is not receptive to having sex.

If low sexual desire is a problem, then you should assess the impact it is having on both partners. Individuals with low desire may not always understand why they have lower desire. This may cause them to feel guilty or inadequate about not having a higher sex drive, perhaps even questioning their masculinity or femininity. Individuals with higher desire may feel hurt and rejected if their partner does not have an interest in sex. They may assume that their partner no longer finds them sexually desirable, perhaps even questioning if their partner loves them. Others will worry that their mate is having an affair or question their mate's sexual orientation, all in an attempt to make sense as to why they have low desire. If individuals rely on sex as a vehicle for achieving closeness, then they may feel emotionally disconnected from their mate.

The general factors that contribute to sexual problems should be evaluated if an individual has low sexual desire. For example, medical and mental health issues need to be ruled out. This is especially true for individuals who previously had an interest in sex, but they have now lost all desire for sex for no apparent reason. For example, depression and the medications used to treat it can both impact desire. Relationship factors also need to be considered given low sexual desire may stem from relationship issues such as conflict or lack of intimacy. Couples can fall into a vicious cycle around their differences in desire (McCarthy & McCarthy, 2014). If the individual with higher desire is critical, angry, or pressures the partner with lower desire for sex, then this can diminish the partner's desire for sex. As the partner's desire decreases, the other becomes increasingly frustrated or angry at the lack of sex in the relationship. This expression of anger only further diminishes the partner's desire for sex, leading to even less sex.

Jackson and Cassidy were caught in this vicious cycle. Early in the couple's marriage, Jackson and Cassidy had a fulfilling sex life. Both experienced strong spontaneous desire for sex, so they would typically have sex four to five times a week on average. However, problems began to arise shortly after the couple experienced a miscarriage. Jackson sought comfort by trying to stay connected to Cassidy. Jackson always felt closest to Cassidy after having sex with her, so he would frequently pursue sex with Cassidy. Unfortunately, Cassidy experienced depression after the miscarriage, which greatly diminished her interest in sex. Therefore, she frequently turned down Jackson's advances for sex. Although Jackson was initially patient with Cassidy's decreased interest in sex, he began to experience greater hurt and frustration over the infrequency in which the couple had intercourse. He began to make angry and critical comments, such as telling Cassidy that she was lucky that he was not having an affair to compensate for the lack of sex in their marriage. Cassidy found these comments insensitive and resented the pressure she felt from Jackson to have sex, which only further reduced her desire for sex.

If a couple is trapped in this vicious cycle, then both will need to make an effort to break free of this cycle (McCarthy & McCarthy, 2014; Weiner Davis, 2003). The mate with higher desire will need to reduce anger and criticism, as well as avoid putting any pressure on the other partner for sex. This may include refraining from initiating sex for a period of time. The mate with higher desire should also attempt to fuel their partner's responsive desire by building motivations for having sex, which can include building emotional connection, offering compliments, providing physical affection without the expectation of sex, or contributing more to childcare or housework.

The individual with lower desire also needs to invest in the couple's sexual relationship. Partners with low sexual desire can do this in a number of ways (Weiner Davis, 2003). Individuals with responsive desire need to remember that they enjoy sex. Initially the individual may not have much desire for sex when first approached, but arousal and desire will build as they begin lovemaking. Also, if individuals notice they are thinking of sex, then they should encourage rather than dismiss those thoughts (much like one will try to start a fire by stoking embers). If they experience any desire for sex, they should act on those feelings. Individuals with low desire also need to learn what their triggers for desire and arousal are, as well as be willing to ask their partner for what they want. In some cases, looking for the exceptions when they do have desire can provide insight on how to build desire.

Male Sexual Disorders

Other problems besides low sexual desire can impact a couple's sex life. Premature ejaculation is a common complaint among men, although not all men who believe they have premature ejaculation actually do based on DSM V criteria (Althof, 2014). According to DSM V criteria, premature ejaculation is diagnosed if there is a recurrent or persistent pattern of ejaculating within 1 minute of sexual intercourse (American Psychiatric Association, 2013). Men without premature ejaculation will typically last 5–10 minutes before ejaculating.

For about two-thirds of men, difficulties with premature ejaculation are lifelong (Althof, 2014). Fortunately, a variety of strategies exist for treating premature ejaculation. Behavioral interventions like the stop-start technique or the squeeze technique have been successfully used to teach men greater ejaculatory control. SSRI antidepressants are also prescribed to treat lifelong premature ejaculation and can extend the time that a man can last before ejaculating.

Another common sexual problem for men is obtaining or maintaining erections (Kalogeropoulus & Larouche, 2020). Erectile difficulties are more likely to be encountered as men age. Erectile difficulties can emerge for a variety of biological (e.g., cardiovascular disease, diabetes) or psychosocial reasons (e.g., performance anxiety). Most men are probably aware that medications like Viagra, Levitra, or Cialis are available to treat erectile problems. These medications are often successful in treating erectile difficulties due to either biological or psychosocial causes. Other treatments (e.g., penile injections, vacuum devices) are available for men who either cannot take the medications (e.g., contraindicated for men taking nitrates) or if the medications are ineffective.

Although less common, some men may have difficulty achieving orgasms, sometimes called delayed ejaculation or male orgasmic disorder (Perelman, 2020). In delayed ejaculation, the man typically has sufficient arousal to achieve erections but insufficient arousal to achieve an orgasm. It will be important to assess what factors impede the man having sufficient arousal to orgasm. These include factors common to other disorders (e.g., inhibitions, performance anxiety, relationship factors), but they may include other factors that create a discrepancy between fantasy and reality (e.g., partner attractiveness, inability to incorporate fetishes). Delayed ejaculation can also be caused by idiosyncratic masturbation practices. The man essentially conditions himself to become aroused and orgasm using techniques that are difficult to replicate in sexual intercourse. Therefore, assessing the man's masturbation practices and fantasies that arouse the man may provide important clues as to why the man has difficulty having an orgasm. Masturbation retraining may be necessary in these situations.

Some men may find that sexual intercourse is painful due to a variety of conditions (Buehler, 2017). For example, sex may be painful for some men who have a significant curvature of the penis as result of Peyroine's disease. Infections of the prostate gland can also lead to painful sex for some men.

Female Sexual Disorders

Like men, women also experience other sexual disorders besides low desire. Some women experience problems having an orgasm (Buehler, 2017; Mintz & Guitelman, 2020). In some cases, they have never experienced an orgasm (primary anorgasmia). Multiple interventions are used to treat primary anorgasmia, including sex education, exploring the woman's anatomy, learning to orgasm through directed masturbation, and then being able to transfer orgasmic patterns into partnered sexual activity.

Many women have difficulty having orgasms through sexual intercourse. Although the woman and her partner may view this as a problem, this is not uncommon. For many women, sexual intercourse does not provide enough stimulation to orgasm, and they must rely on oral or manual stimulation for orgasm. For women seeking to achieve an orgasm during sexual intercourse, they may need to experiment with a number of things, including extending foreplay and using positions that provide more clitoral stimulation. For example, the coital alignment technique is one position that provides greater clitoral stimulation. The couple may also want to use positions that allow for simultaneous penetration and manual stimulation of the clitoris.

Many women experience painful intercourse, a condition called dyspareunia (Bergeron et al., 2020). It is important that women seek medical evaluation for dyspareunia because it is often due to a medical condition (e.g., infections of the vulva or vagina, fibroid tumors, endometriosis). Women may also experience painful sex after menopause due to having less secretions and the thinning of the vaginal walls. Like other pain disorders, cognitive behavioral therapy may be helpful in coping with dyspareunia, especially if the underlying cause of the pain cannot be identified and treated.

Some women experience vaginismus, a condition where the outer muscles of the vagina constrict, making penetration of the vagina impossible (ter Kuile & Reissing, 2020). Vaginismus requires specialized treatment where the woman learns relaxation techniques in combination with using dilators of increasing size so that she can eventually tolerate penetration by a penis. If vaginismus developed as a result of dyspareunia, then this also needs to be treated.

Protective Factors in a Sexual Relationship

Couples can do several different things to help protect or maintain a healthy sexual relationship. By assessing for these protective factors, you may be able to identify possible strengths in the couple's sexual relationship. Conversely, an absence of these factors could point to areas where the couple may need help to strengthen their sexual relationship.

Integrate Emotional Intimacy With Sex

Sex in the beginning of a relationship is fueled by strong romantic feelings. However, it is natural that the intensity of these feelings will decline with time. McCarthy and McCarthy (2014) observe that couples in long-term relationships need to learn how to integrate intimacy with eroticism. Intimate sexuality requires "dealing with the whole person and sharing the complexities of your lives, including emotional and sexual intimacy" (p. 38). This intimate sexuality can be equally (if not more) fulfilling, but in a different way.

Emotional Connection and Intimacy

Consistent with the previous point, maintaining a strong emotional connection is important to enhancing one's sexual intimacy (McCarthy & McCarthy, 2014) Maintaining a strong emotional connection can be especially important for partners with strong responsive desire. Couples who learn to speak each other's love languages and are intentional in spending quality time together will be able to build and sustain a strong emotional bond (see Chapter 7). Strengthening intimacy (see Chapter 3) can also deepen the emotional connection.

Sensuality and Physical Affection

Promoting sensuality through physical touch can also enhance a couple's sexual relationship (McCarthy & McCarthy, 2014; Markman et al., 2010). Couples with a healthy sexual relationship consistently provide their partner physical affection in several ways. This includes things such as holding hands, hugging, cuddling, kissing, or a sensual massage. Physical touch can help build a desire for sex. However, it is also important that physical affection is not always viewed as a prelude to sex, but it is something that is enjoyed and appreciated in itself.

Ability to Communicate About Sex

You also should assess a couple's ability to talk about sex with one another. Couples who can talk about sex will be better able to communicate their sexual needs. For example, couples need an agreed upon way to initiate and refuse sex (J. M. Gottman & J. S. Gottman, 2015). They also need to be able to share with their partners the things that turn them on or turn them off sexually (Markman et al., 2010; McCarthy & McCarthy, 2014).

Engage in a Variety of Sexual Behaviors

Couples also need to be able to engage in a variety of sexual behaviors to keep their sexual relationship fresh and exciting (J. M. Gottman & J. S. Gottman, 2015; Markman et al., 2010; McCarthy & McCarthy, 2014). Boredom will set in if the couple always engages in sex in the same way. Therefore, it can be helpful to assess if the couple incorporates creativity and novelty in their sexual relationship rather than following a narrow or rigid script in terms of sex.

Pornography

Pornography is a complex issue. Some couples view pornography as a normal and acceptable means to enhance sexual desire. These couples do not see pornography use by either partner or as a couple as a problem. However, other couples may find that pornography negatively impacts their sexual relationship, particularly if one partner objects to the other's use of pornography.

If pornography is an issue in the relationship, then a careful assessment must be made to determine why it is problematic. Pornography use can create a problem in relationships in two ways. First, the couple may have different views on whether it is appropriate to use pornography.

One individual may use pornography and view it as normative behavior. However, the other partner may view pornography as morally objectionable or wrong. The couple's different values regarding pornography can create differing expectations regarding whether it is appropriate to use, creating a contract issue (see Chapter 9) for the couple that needs to be resolved.

Problems can also arise if one partner uses pornography excessively (Maltz & Maltz, 2010). Some individuals consume considerable time and money looking at pornography, which can leave their partner feeling hurt, neglected, angry, or resentful. In some cases, individuals may put their jobs or careers at risk by looking at pornography at work. For some individuals, pornography may begin to impact their sexual functioning. If the individual can only be aroused with certain stimuli through pornography, then the individual may experience problems during sex with a partner, such as low desire, erectile difficulties, or difficulty achieving an orgasm. Excessive use can also shape an individual's sexual taste in pornography over time. As individuals become habituated to certain types of pornography, they may search for more extreme forms of pornography in their search for more novel and arousing depictions of sex. In some cases, this can lead to illegal behavior if the individual begins to consume pornography that depicts minors. Therefore, your assessment should include how often the individual uses pornography, the type of pornography that is typically consumed, and the potential impact the pornography use may have upon the individual's sexual functioning (e.g., desire, arousal).

Exploring several areas can help you identify why pornography is an issue in the relationship. Assessment of the individual who uses pornography can center on several elements. How does the individual who uses pornography view the behavior? Doug sees his use of pornography as nonproblematic and something that all men do. In contrast, Joel sees his infrequent use of pornography as problematic because any use of pornography is against his and his wife's religious beliefs. As noted above, it is important to consider the frequency of pornography use. A high level of usage may indicate a potential problem. Why does the individual use pornography? Does it simply provide a means of increasing arousal, or does it serve some other function? For example, some individuals use pornography to cope with negative emotions, which can lead to a vicious cycle. Joel often uses pornography to cope with his depression because it provides a distraction from his mood and makes him feel temporarily better. However, because pornography is against his religious values, he feels guilty whenever he uses it. This guilt, in turn, magnifies his depression and makes him vulnerable again to using pornography.

It is also important to assess the partner's view of the mate's pornography use. Why does the partner object to the individual's pornography use? Does the partner object to any use of pornography, or would it be allowable in some situations? For example, Joel's wife Delores found pornography morally objectionable and often denigrating to women. Therefore, she did not feel that Joel using pornography was acceptable under any circumstance. In contrast, Janice was uncomfortable when Doug used pornography to masturbate by himself because she felt this was a substitute for them having partnered sex. Yet, Janice was open to the use of pornography if it was used as part of the couple's foreplay.

It can also be important to consider the impact the mate's pornography use has upon the partner. Some women (and men) report that their mate using pornography makes them feel unattractive or insecure about their bodies because they cannot compete with the individuals depicted in pornography. A mate's pornography use can also trigger negative feelings associated with prior sexual abuse or assault. The partner may also fear that the mate prefers masturbating to pornography versus having sex with the partner.

You should also assess relationship dynamics around the pornography issue. Couples are at risk for developing vicious cycles around pornography use. If one mate continues to use pornography despite the partner's objections, then conflict can obviously arise. The mate may try to hide their pornography use to avoid conflict. However, the secrecy around using pornography can add to the sense of betrayal, further magnifying the conflict. In another common vicious cycle, partners who find their mate's pornography use objectionable may begin to have less desire for sex. As sex diminishes between the couple, the mate may depend more on masturbating to pornography to meet sexual needs.

Maltz and Maltz (2010) recommend that individuals take six action steps if they are struggling with pornography use and would like to stop. First, they need to tell someone about the problem to break the isolation and secrecy that can help maintain pornography use. Second, individuals should get involved in some form of treatment. Some pursue individual therapy, while others join groups that focus on sexual addictions or compulsions (e.g., various 12-step groups, Smart Recovery). Third, individuals need to create a porn-free environment. For example, computer software can be installed that limits access to pornographic sites. Fourth, individuals need to create a network of people who will provide 24-hour support and accountability for not using pornography. Fifth, individuals need to learn how to take care of their physical and emotional health given that stress in these areas can trigger pornography use. Finally, individuals need to develop healthy attitudes and behaviors regarding sex, including developing an intimacy-based approach to sex.

Conclusion

Sex is an important element of caring. Due to the complex nature of assessing and treating sexual problems, a separate chapter has been devoted to this topic. It is important that therapists ask about sex given that many couples may experience problems in this area, but they may hesitate to disclose this to their therapist. Table 8.1 offers a list of questions that will aid you in doing an effective assessment of a couple's sexual functioning. The questions reflect the need to conduct an assessment using a biopsychosocial perspective.

Table 8.1 General Assessment Questions for Sex

Sexual History

1. If a sexual disorder is present, is it lifelong (primary) or acquired (secondary)? If acquired, when did the problem arise?
2. Is the sexual disorder situational or generalizable? Are there any exceptions as to when the sexual problem does not exist?
3. Is there any history of sexual trauma?
4. Does the individual have any inhibitions?
5. Does the individual have any negative or unrealistic beliefs about sex?
6. What is the individual's sexual orientation?
7. Does the individual have any unusual sexual preferences (e.g., paraphilias)?

(Continued)

Table 8.1 (Continued)

Masturbation

1. Does the individual masturbate, and with what frequency?
2. Does the sexual disorder exist during masturbation?
3. How does the individual masturbate (e.g., idiosyncratic approach)?
4. What types of fantasies or materials arouse the individual during masturbation?

Current Sexual Encounters

1. Does the individual experience performance anxiety before or during sex?
2. How narrow or broad is the couple's sexual script?
3. How does the individual try to manage the problem during sex?
4. How does the partner respond to the individual's sexual problem during sex?
5. Does the individual's sexual problem impact the partner's sexual functioning in any way?

Relationship Factors

1. Is the individual experiencing any problems in their relationship?
2. Do relationship problems (e.g., conflict, emotional distance, affair) contribute to the individual's sexual difficulties?
3. What is the impact of the sexual disorder on the couple's sexual or relationship satisfaction?
4. How does the partner make sense of the individual's sex problem?
5. What impact does the sexual disorder have on the partner?
6. Does the partner have a sexual disorder?
7. How openly can the couple communicate about sex?

Mental Health

1. What are stressors in the individual's life? Are they impacting sexual functioning?
2. Does the individual have any mental health disorders (e.g., depression, anxiety) that may impact sexual functioning?
3. Is the individual taking any medications (e.g., SSRI antidepressants) for mental health issues that may be impacting sexual functioning?
4. Is the individual using any substances (e.g., alcohol, drugs) that may be impacting sexual functioning?

Physical Health

1. Does the individual have any medical illnesses or physical conditions that may be impacting sexual functioning (e.g., diabetes)?

2. Is the individual taking any medications to treat medical issues that may be impacting sexual functioning?

Pornography (if applicable)

1. Is the use of pornography a problem in the relationship?

2. How does the individual view their use of pornography (e.g., normative, against personal values)?

3. How frequently does the individual use pornography? What type of pornography does the individual consume?

4. What factors contribute to the individual using pornography (e.g., arousal, cope with negative emotions)?

5. Why does the partner find the mate's use of pornography problematic (e.g., different values, excessive use, type of pornography)?

6. What impact does the mate's use of pornography have on the partner?

7. What are the relationship dynamics (e.g., vicious cycles) around the issue of pornography?

9

CONTRACT

In this chapter we will explore how contract problems can arise in intimate relationships. In business, a contract is a written or spoken agreement between two parties that specifies what is expected of the other. Defined in this manner, a contract also exists between two people in an intimate relationship. Consciously or unconsciously, individuals hold expectations about how their partner will behave toward them or in the relationship (Markman et al., 2010). Some expectations can be very general or broad, such as the expectation that the partner will be faithful, loving, or committed to the relationship. Other expectations might be more concrete and specific, such as who cuts the lawn, who pays the bills, the frequency in which the couple has sex, or how much money one can spend without consulting the other. The compilation of these various expectations constitutes the couple's contract.

Unlike most business contracts, relationship contracts are seldom spelled out in writing. The one exception might be a prenuptial

DOI: 10.4324/9781003161967-9

agreement. In fact, some expectations may never be spoken of directly, even though they still shape what the partners expect of each other. For example, some couples may never explicitly discuss the expectation that they will each remain sexually faithful, but this expectation still exists.

Problems around a couple's contract can emerge in four ways. First, couples may not have clearly articulated their expectations with one another. As a result, each partner may not fully know what each expects of the other, which can lead to problems. Second, as couples begin to define the expectations, they may discover that they have different expectations about the relationship that need to be ironed out. Third, even if a couple works out an acceptable contract initially in their relationship, changes or new circumstances may require the couple to renegotiate their contract. Finally, some couples must also deal with breaches in their contract, such as infidelity or other acts of betrayal. Assessment of each of these potential contract issues is the focus of this chapter.

Contract Issue One – Unstated Expectations

Couples may experience contract problems early in their relationship that arise from not having clearly articulated their expectations with one another (Markman et al., 2010). Unstated expectations increase the chances that each of them will miss the mark in meeting their partner's needs because they do not know exactly what those needs are. Sometimes this disappointment will spark conflict for a couple.

Expectations may be unstated for a variety of reasons. In some cases, individuals may assume their partner is working from a similar set of expectations. Therefore, there is not the perceived need to make the expectations explicit. In other cases, some expectations are never discussed because individuals may not be consciously aware of them. Individuals can internalize certain beliefs about how relationships should be (or not be) based on what they have learned from their families of origin, other personal relationships, or their culture (Markman et al., 2010). These beliefs may operate outside their immediate awareness, yet they can powerfully inform what they expect from their partner in the relationship. Individuals may not be aware that they hold a particular expectation of their partner until it is violated in some way. Another reason an expectation may be left unstated is if there is embarrassment or shame attached to it. For example, individuals may be reluctant to share their expectations regarding sex due to their embarrassment or shame in regard to sex.

The most obvious solution to this problem is to make every effort to uncover and make explicit each other's expectations (Markman et al., 2010). Ideally, couples will be proactive in discussing expectations early in the relationship. However, most couples encounter some conflict over unclear expectations as they learn more about one another. Viewed in a positive light, conflict at this early stage can be viewed as an opportunity to discover unstated expectations.

How can couples be proactive in identifying expectations? One way to do this is to take an inventory that explores topics important to relationship success. For example, most couples preparing for marriage find taking a premarital inventory like PREPARE, FOCCUS, or RELATE helpful in exploring their relationship to uncover their expectations. Both PREPARE and FOCCUS require a trained facilitator to administer and go over the results with the couple. If you are not a trained facilitator, couples can find one through the websites for both PREPARE (www.prepare-enrich.com) and FOCCUS (www.foccusinc. com). After the couple completes the inventory, the results are sent to the facilitator, who provides feedback and facilitates a discussion of the results with the couples. In contrast to PREPARE and FOCCUS, couples can go directly to the RELATE website (https://relateinstitute. com/the-relate-assessment) to sign up to take the inventory and get their results directly.

The premarital inventories provide couples feedback on how they are doing in a number of areas important to marriage. However, engaged couples should be encouraged not to view the results as a test that they must pass to see if they should get married or not. Rather, the results should be used as a springboard for couples to discuss and explore many different elements of their relationship. For example, having individuals share why they responded to a question in the manner that they did can generate a deeper understanding of each other, which can strengthen the couple's connection. As noted earlier, it can also uncover unstated expectations that the couple can discuss and address.

Contract Issue Two – Negotiating Different Expectations

Sometimes couples have made their expectations clear with one another, but they have different expectations about how the relationship should operate. For example, couples may differ on their expectations around closeness and autonomy in a relationship. These differing expectations have the potential to create conflict in the relationship. Hiebert et al. (1993, p. 101) refer to this set of expectations as relationship blueprints. When couples have different expectations or blueprints for the relationship, there is the potential for a power struggle or "blueprint war" to emerge as each partner fights for their vision of what the relationship should look like.

If a couple is caught in conflict over different expectations, then you can help the couple step back and ask themselves several important questions. First, why is the expectation important for each individual? Sometimes understanding the origins of the expectation can help individuals understand its importance. As noted earlier, expectations can be shaped by experiences in individuals' families of origin, previous experiences, or cultural backgrounds (Markman et al., 2010). For example, Allison, a devout Catholic, was very upset that Tristan did not go to the midnight Christmas Mass with her. Even though Allison knew that Tristan was not religious and questioned whether God existed, it was still important to her that they attend the Christmas Mass together. When asked why this was so important to her, Allison began to cry and said that she had fond memories of her family celebrating Christmas together, including their tradition of going to midnight Christmas Mass. When Tristan decided not to go to church with her, Allison was upset and sad because she wanted that same connection with Tristan that she had with her family growing up. Once Tristan understood the importance behind Allison's expectation, he promised to go with her next year.

Second, are the expectations realistic or reasonable? Not all of our expectations are (Markman et al., 2010). When Tovio came to therapy, he stated that he didn't think that he and his wife should have any more disagreements after therapy was over. His wife Leah immediately challenged him by saying that she did not see this as a realistic expectation because all couples have disagreements, even happily married ones. Sometimes it is not realistic to expect that our mate will be able to change to fulfill our expectations. What individuals perceive as an unwillingness to change may in reality be an inability to change because it is just part of their mate's nature. Thus, individuals must accept it as part of who their partner is, along with the other positive qualities that they love.

Third, is compromise possible? If not, then individuals may be left with a difficult choice. Is the expectation important enough to the individual that it is a deal breaker, or can the individual live with this expectation unfulfilled? This was the dilemma that Craig and Britney faced regarding whether or not to have children. When the couple got married, both knew that they had different expectations regarding having children. Britney came from a large family and always wanted children. However, Craig was not interested in being a father. When the couple got married, Britney had health issues that prevented her from becoming pregnant. So, the couple's disagreement over whether to have children was put on the back burner in the early years of the marriage. However, as Britney resolved her health issues and was entering her late 30s, her desire to start a family became pressing. The impasse over whether to have a child was the issue that brought the couple into therapy.

Britney's desire to have a child was very strong. Although she loved Craig, she could not imagine never being a mother. It became clear that if Craig were unwilling to have children, this would be a deal breaker for Britney and that she would leave the relationship to pursue her dream of being a mother with another partner. Craig also had to explore whether having children was a deal breaker for him or something that he could agree to pursue. When the therapist asked Craig why he did not want children, he acknowledged that there was actually a part of him that wanted to be a father, but he had two big fears that prevented him from wanting children. The first fear that Craig expressed was a fear that there was a strong possibility that Britney would die during childbirth. To help Craig evaluate how realistic this was, the therapist asked Craig to do research to determine the actual probability of women dying during childbirth. Although Craig found that death through childbirth was still a possibility, he discovered that he had greatly overestimated the probability of this happening. Doing research helped quell his fears around this. His second fear was related to his own family of origin experience of losing his own father as an adolescent. Being significantly older than

Britney, Craig had a fear that he would die before his child became an adult. This fear was explored in therapy, including the probability this could happen and what it might mean if the couple pursued having a child and his fear did indeed come true. Eventually, Craig decided that his fears should not prevent him from having a child, especially if it meant losing his wife.

For compromise to be successful, you should evaluate several elements with the couple. First, is each person willing to make some concessions to find an acceptable compromise? Couples can remain locked in conflict over contradictory expectations if each insists that their expectations be fully met. This puts the couple in a situation where one will be a winner and the other a loser. The goal of compromise is to find a middle ground where each gives up a bit, but the couple ultimately feels that their most important needs are met. This creates a win-win solution for both parties.

Second, is the amount that each is willing to compromise equitable? If one person must concede a lot more than the other, then the compromise may not feel fair to one person. How much one is willing to concede can depend upon the situation. In some situations, some individuals may be willing to concede more than their partner, especially if the issue is not as important to them as it is to the partner. This may be workable in specific situations provided that this person is not always the one compromising more. However, if there is a pattern where one partner consistently concedes more than the other, then resentment can build because it feels unbalanced overall. This was the case for Sampson and Carl. Sampson often had strong opinions about what the couple should be doing, such as where to eat, what movies to see, or where to vacation. Carl, who was more laid back, would often go along with what Sampson wanted to avoid conflict and because he often did not feel as strongly about it as Sampson did. However, over time, Carl began to resent that the relationship seemed primarily oriented toward what Sampson wanted. Therapy focused on how to bring greater balance to the couple's relationship.

Third, how do power dynamics in the relationship impact the couple's ability to negotiate an equitable compromise? If the power is imbalanced in the relationship, then one person may be at a significant disadvantage in influencing the other person (Knudson-Martin, 2013). Claudia, who was a stay-at-home mother for the couple's 3-year-old twins, felt like she had less power in the relationship with her husband Andrew because he worked outside the home and provided all the family's income. Especially when it came to financial decisions, Claudia felt like she had to defer more to what Andrew wanted.

Finally, you should assess if both partners feel that their most essential needs are being met. If individuals feel that their most important needs are being compromised, then the solution is less likely to be successful. The Gottman approach (J. M. Gottman & J. S. Gottman, 2015) recommends couples do a two-circle exercise when attempting to problem-solve through compromise. Each partner draws a large circle on the outside, and a smaller circle inside. Each partner is then asked to consider what their wants and needs are in regard to the problem. Each person's needs are placed in the inner circle, which will ideally not be sacrificed to find a suitable compromise. The individual's wants are placed in the outer circle, which are preferences that can be flexibly negotiated in an attempt to find a workable compromise.

Contract Issue Three – Renegotiating Contracts

Sometimes couples have problems because they need to renegotiate aspects of their contracts, especially at important transitions in their lives. Examples of these transitions may include having children, returning to school, changing careers, or retiring. Couples who previously had a workable contract can sometimes become stuck as they renegotiate a new contract. For example, Glen and Gloria came to therapy over conflict in the relationship over household chores. The conflict had recently arisen after Glen retired. Gloria stated that she wanted Glen to help out more with housework now that he had retired and had more free time. However, Glen replied that he did not retire so he could do housework.

A major illness or injury to one of the partners may also force a couple to renegotiate their contract. Brad was seriously injured in a cycling accident, and thus he was unable to continue working due to his injuries. Alexis, who had been a stay-at-home mother for their two young sons, obtained a full-time job to replace Brad's lost income. However, she felt resentment that she could no longer be a stay-at-home mother, and greatly missed the time she previously had with her sons.

You can help couples renegotiate their contract utilizing many of the suggestions stated in the earlier sections on contract. Couples are encouraged to uncover and state their expectations. It is also helpful if the couple can explore the importance and origin of their expectations, and if a suitable compromise can be reached if necessary.

Contract Issue Four – Dealing With a Breach of Contract

Another contract issue that can arise for a couple is a breach of contract. In other words, one partner has done something to seriously violate the contract. The most common example would be when someone has an affair, although breaches of the contract can occur in other ways. For example, feeling abandoned at a critical time of need (e.g., miscarriage, delivery of a baby, serious illness) can violate one's expectation that their partner will be there in a time of need. A perceived breach of contract can also occur if one partner asks to renegotiate an important part of the contract that the other feels was foundational to their original contract. For example, Darnell and Shaniqua agreed early in their relationship that they would always live in the Chicago area to be close to both extended families. However, the company that Darnell worked for offered him a significant promotion and pay raise if he was willing to relocate to the west coast to work in another office. Darnell was excited about the new position and promotion, and he was willing to move his family to California for the new job opportunity. However, Shaniqua was upset that Darnell was putting pressure on her to move across the country and be away from their extended families. Shaniqua felt betrayed because she thought this was a non-negotiable and permanent part of their relationship contract.

How do you deal with a situation where one partner feels hurt by a breach of contract, such as an infidelity? Addressing the 6 As discussed next can facilitate the couple healing from the injury to the relationship (Williams et al., 2011). The 6 As can be a template for working through any type of injury, although the work required to address each A will be more extensive if the injury is serious like an affair.

Apology

Has an apology been made? When one person has hurt another, it is often expected that the individual will offer an apology to the hurt partner. However, many individuals find it difficult to apologize because it requires directly admitting to having done something wrong, which can be embarrassing or even humiliating depending upon the nature of the offense. For small transgressions, a simple apology may be sufficient to heal the relationship. However, for more serious injuries, incorporating the other A's below into the apology will be necessary to adequately address the breach of contract.

Accept Responsibility

Has the individual accepted responsibility for their actions? An apology is more powerful if the individual takes full responsibility for injuring the partner. Making excuses or blaming the other person can undermine or discount an apology. For example, Thomas blamed Roxanne for his affair, claiming that he would not have had an affair if Roxanne had been more sexually available. Blaming her for the affair made it difficult for Roxanne to forgive Thomas for his infidelity. In contrast, Anthony told his wife Stacy that regardless of the reasons why he had the affair, he was ultimately responsible for his actions.

Acknowledge Hurt

Is the individual able to clearly articulate how they have hurt their partner? An apology is much more effective if the individual can clearly state how the injured partner was affected. For serious injuries, the hurt partner may be impacted in a number of ways. During the course of therapy, Anthony learned the variety of ways in which Stacy had been negatively impacted by his affair. For example, Anthony was able to acknowledge how she felt hurt and betrayed, how difficult it was to lose a sense of safety in the relationship, the damage to her self-esteem, and how she felt humiliated by the discovery of the affair by friends and family members. The more clearly Anthony was able to state the impact his infidelity had upon Stacy, the more sincere she felt his remorse was for the affair.

Answer Why

Has the partner offered an explanation for why they behaved in the way they did? For serious betrayals like an infidelity, the hurt partner will want to understand why their partner acted in the manner in which they did. Answering why is especially important if the hurt partner believes that the partner's actions are a sign that they do not love them. Typically, this is not the case, and the actions are driven by other factors. For example, when Danilo came to therapy, he admitted to having an affair with a young woman while visiting his family in the Philippines. Danilo said he loved his wife Marisol and wanted to heal his marriage. As Danilo shared his story of how the affair happened, multiple factors were uncovered that contributed to the affair. During his extended visit, Danilo began to feel somewhat lonely and began to socialize with a young woman he met. Danilo admitted to being flattered by the young woman's attention, which was a boost to his low self-esteem. Cultural factors also played a role. Danilo admitted that the young woman likely sought out the affair as a way to escape an impoverished background. Danilo explained that young women in the Philippines will sometimes seek to become mistresses of wealthy men to escape poverty. Danilo admitted that this was likely the reason the woman initially sought him out. The young woman asked Danilo if he would set her up in an apartment so he could visit her in secret, which he agreed to do.

Answering why is also important to rebuild trust. If the individual cannot state why they acted as they did, then the hurt partner will wonder what is to prevent the partner from doing the same thing again. Thus, uncovering reasons for affairs or other serious injuries requires careful exploration. Typically, the reasons for an affair defy a simple explanation and require identifying multiple factors that contributed to the affair.

Atonement

What changes is the individual making to avoid injuring the partner again? This question reflects the concept of atonement, which refers to the actions that individuals take to demonstrate their remorse and prevent their partner from being injured again. What atonement looks like will vary from situation to situation. For example, a person's atonement should reflect one of the key reasons the individual had an affair.

If low self-esteem is a key factor behind the affair, then uncovering and addressing the underlying causes for the low self-esteem could be how the individual shows atonement. Thus, answering why the injury happened often informs what is the most effective form of atonement.

Accumulate Trust

What steps is the individual taking to build trust with their partner? When a serious injury has happened, it may be very difficult to rebuild trust in the relationship. Trust can be slowly accumulated over time if the individual makes appropriate efforts to address the A's previously described. For example, being willing to talk about an affair and explore why it happened is important to rebuilding trust. Atonement also demonstrates the individual's desire to heal the relationship and make it a priority, which can also help rebuild trust.

It is important to recognize that accumulating or rebuilding trust after a serious injury can take time, and both parties need to be patient with the process. Being impatient with the hurt partner's ability to forgive the infidelity can be perceived as an invalidation of the partner's pain, which may interfere with the healing process.

For couples who have experienced a breach of contract, it can be helpful to assess where the couple is at in terms of completing each of the above tasks required for healing. After describing each A, you can then ask each individual to rank on a scale from 1 to 10 how successful they have been in addressing each A. It is important to ask each individual what rating they would give because their perspectives may differ. Significantly different ratings may indicate a potential stuck point in the healing. Low scores on any of the tasks will also need to be addressed, which may require further assessment. For example, couples often report little insight as to why an affair happened. Therefore, you will want to learn more about the affair so you can help the couple identify the ingredients that led to the affair.

Conclusion

This chapter has explored the importance of looking at expectations in a relationship, which form the basis for a couple's contract. These expectations can be explicit or unspoken, as well as general or specific.

Couples who have not made many of their expectations explicit may experience conflict through unmet expectations. As therapists, we can help couples uncover and discuss these expectations, sometimes using tools like premarital inventories. Sometimes couples have important differences in their expectations, which can also create conflict. As therapists, we may need to help couples explore the importance and source of these expectations, as well as if there is room for compromise. In some cases, couples may need to renegotiate their contract if there have been changes in their lives due to significant life events or transitions. Finally, as therapists we may be called upon to help couples heal an important breach of their contract, such as an affair. Using the 6 As as a framework, we can help couples assess where they are stuck in the healing process. Table 9.1 provides a summary of the key assessment questions that you should consider as you examine a couple's contract.

Table 9.1 Assessment of Contract Issues

The following questions can be used to help assess a couple's strengths and areas of growth in terms of their relationship contract:

1. Has the couple clearly articulated their expectations to one another, or are there important expectations that have not been uncovered and shared? (Note: For engaged couples, using a premarital inventory may be an excellent assessment tool for uncovering expectations.)

2. Does the couple have conflicting expectations in any important areas that are creating issues or conflict? If so, additional questions to explore may include:

    a. Why is the expectation important to each individual?

    b. Where did the expectation come from (e.g., family of origin, a previous relationship, cultural background)?

    c. Is the expectation realistic or reasonable?

    d. Is compromise possible, or is the issue a deal breaker? If compromise is possible: Is each willing to compromise? Is the amount of compromise each is doing in the relationship equitable? How do power dynamics influence the couple's ability to negotiate an equitable compromise? Are individuals able to find a compromise without sacrificing important needs?

(Continued)

Table 9.1 (Continued)

3. Have any significant changes, transitions, or events precipitated the need for the couple to renegotiate their contract? If so, have these new expectations been stated? Is the couple in agreement with the changes in expectations?

4. Has someone caused a significant injury (i.e., breach in the couple's contract) that needs to be healed? If so, have the following tasks been accomplished?

    a. Has the person who created the injury apologized?

    b. Has the person who created the injury accepted full responsibility for their actions?

    c. Has the person who created the injury been able to fully acknowledge how they have hurt their partner?

    d. Has the person who created the injury been able to answer why they committed the action (e.g., infidelity)?

    e. Has the person who created the injury demonstrated atonement for their actions?

    f. Has the person who created the injury taken the necessary steps to help build trust again (e.g., transparency)?

10

CHARACTER

The seventh C, character, refers to the individual attributes that each person brings into the relationship. This chapter will focus on four primary domains that relate to character. The first section will focus on personality, which can be both an asset and a liability for relationships. For example, differences in personality may be one of the reasons that the partners were attracted to each other initially. At the same time, differences in personality can be the basis for perpetual problems (see Chapter 4) that the couple must somehow manage. The second section will look at the importance of assessing for emotional sensitivities that individuals may bring into the relationship. The third section examines the potential challenges that physical or mental illness may place on relationships, as well as possible strategies couples might utilize to cope with them. The fourth and final section will emphasize the need to uncover the strengths of each partner. Each individual possesses personal qualities or attributes that can enrich the relationship.

DOI: 10.4324/9781003161967-10

Personality

Individuals often have elements of their character that are relatively stable and not likely to change dramatically. These character features are related to the person's personality. For example, some people have more outgoing personalities, while others are more reserved when it comes to socializing with new people.

The combination of each person's personality can create unique advantages and disadvantages for each couple. For example, differences in personality can be the basis for attraction, but they can also be a potential source of conflict for couples. When Julio met Zoe, he was attracted to her free spirit and playful side. In contrast, Julio frequently focused on his responsibilities, setting goals for himself each day to accomplish. Julio prized himself for being a highly organized and conscientious individual. Julio initially enjoyed the fun and spontaneity that Zoe introduced into his life. Zoe, for her part, was attracted to how grounded Julio seemed to be as a person. Growing up in a chaotic family, Zoe liked how Julio seemed to live a stable life. When the couple began to live together, conflict began to emerge for the couple. Julio felt that Zoe was sometimes irresponsible, often prioritizing pleasurable activities over her chores and other responsibilities. Zoe felt resentful of the expectations that Julio placed on her and encouraged Julio to "loosen up." When the couple came into therapy, the therapist recognized that the couple was struggling over differences in personality. The therapist helped the couple recognize that their differences created a perpetual problem (see Chapter 4) that would require greater acceptance from each.

This section will provide a brief overview of the two popular approaches for understanding personality, the Big Five personality traits and the Myers-Briggs. However, be aware that there are other approaches to conceptualizing and assessing personality (e.g., 16 Personality Factor Questionnaire, Enneagram, Eysenck Personality Inventory, HEXACO Personality Inventory, Taylor Johnson Temperament Analysis) that will not be covered.

The Big Five

The Big Five model is a widely accepted model in psychology for understanding personality (Goldberg, 1993; John et al., 2008; McCrae &

Oliver, 1992). As the name implies, an individual's personality is based on five different dimensions, which are openness, conscientiousness, extraversion, agreeableness, and neuroticism. Each dimension is seen as a continuum, with each person falling somewhere between the two extreme ends of the spectrum.

People who score high on the openness dimension seek out new experiences and ideas. They often have traits such as being creative, artistic, imaginative, and curious. Individuals low in openness prefer the known to the unknown, such as familiar places, routines, or people. Their thinking is also more conventional and concrete in comparison to those high in openness.

Individuals high on conscientiousness value self-discipline (e.g., delay gratification), acting responsibly, being dependable, and accomplishing goals. They also like structure, organization, and having a plan. In contrast, individuals lower in conscientiousness prefer spontaneity and flexibility rather than following a plan. At an extreme, individuals low in conscientiousness can be impulsive, lazy, careless, aimless, and unreliable.

Individuals who score high on extraversion seek stimulation through the external world, often through interacting with people. Therefore, they tend to be highly social people. They also seek energy by engaging in stimulating activities. In contrast, those who score low on this dimension (introverts) seek less stimulation from the external world, and need more time alone compared to those high on the extraversion scale. They also tend to be more reserved in social situations compared to extraverts.

People high on agreeableness value getting along with other people. Consistent with this, they show several traits such as being kind, cooperative, compassionate, and having a desire to help others. They tend to see the positive in people, and they are generally trusting and tolerant of others. In contrast, individuals low in agreeableness can be unfriendly, argumentative, competitive, show little interest in the needs of others, and be manipulative.

Neuroticism measures an individual's tendency to experience negative emotions such as sadness, anger, anxiety, or depression. Individuals who score high on neuroticism are more pessimistic and easily upset by stress. In contrast, those who score low on neuroticism are calmer and less likely to experience negative emotions.

A number of instruments have been developed to measure personality using the Big Five (Fetvadjiev & van de Vijver, 2015), including the Big Five Inventory (BFI), the Big Five Questionnaire (BFQ), the Five Factor Personality Inventory (FFPI), and the NEO Personality Inventory, Revised (NEO PI-R). A free version of the Big Five Inventory (BFI) can be found at www.outofservice.com/bigfive.

The Myers-Briggs

The Myers-Briggs is another approach to understanding personality. Many people have heard of the Myers-Briggs because of its popularity. The Myers-Briggs has four dimensions, which include extraversion (E) or introversion (I), sensing (S) or intuition (N), thinking (T) or feeling (F), and judging (J) or perceiving (P).

Similar to what was described for the extraversion dimension the Big Five, extraverts are focused on deriving stimulation from the external world through action and interacting with people. In contrast, introverts are more drawn to the inner world, contemplating concepts and ideas. They are generally more reserved socially compared to extraverts, instead enjoying solitary time and privacy.

Individuals who are sensors focus on their senses when observing the world. Sensors tend to focus on the here and now, are good with facts and details, and view themselves as practical or pragmatic. In contrast, intuitive individuals value following hunches or intuition, looking beyond what is directly visible or evident to the senses. They are also more concerned about future possibilities rather than the present, focus on the big picture versus the details, and prefer dealing with ideas rather than facts.

Thinkers and feelers approach decision-making differently. Thinkers make decisions using logic or analytical thinking, and value being fair and objective in decision-making. In contrast, feelers make decisions based more on how it will impact others. They are more likely to make decisions to maintain harmony in relationships and are willing to take into account special circumstances or needs.

Judgers like organization, structure, and following a plan. In contrast, perceivers prefer to go with the flow and be spontaneous. Judgers seek closure through making decisions, whereas perceivers may be hesitant to make firm decisions because they like things open-ended. Judgers and perceivers also differ in their orientations to work and play. Judgers typically want to complete their work before they allow themselves to play, whereas perceivers have no difficulty in postponing some of their responsibilities to protect time to play.

The Myers-Briggs Type Indicator can be taken through a certified administrator or is available online (www.mbtionline.com). Some individuals prefer to use the Keirsey Temperament Sorter because it is a significantly shorter instrument than the Myers-Briggs Type Indicator. The Keirsey Temperament Sorter can be found in the book *Please Understand Me II* (Keirsey, 1998) or online (www.keirsey.com). Although the Keirsey Temperament Sorter and Myers-Briggs Type Indicator take somewhat different approaches to measuring and conceptualizing how the dimensions relate to one another, both can be useful in identifying personality types. In many cases, clinical observation and follow-up questions may be sufficient to identify and confirm key differences on one or more of the dimensions. Therefore, it may not always be necessary for a couple to take a formal assessment using the Keirsey Temperament Sorter and Myers-Briggs Type Indicator, especially if the couple is quite different on one or more dimensions.

Which Is Best?

In presenting both the Big Five and the Myers-Briggs, a question that might arise is which one is the best to use? An argument can be made for both. Indeed, there is some overlap between the Big Five and the Myers-Briggs in terms of dimensions. From an empirical standpoint, the Big Five has a stronger reputation than the Myers-Briggs. Another advantage of the Big Five is that the five dimensions are on a continuum rather than in categories, which more accurately reflects that people differ to the degree they have a particular trait.

In contrast to the Big Five, individuals who use the Myers-Briggs will report they are one type or the other (e.g., extravert versus introvert). However, like the Big Five, it is probably best to think of each dimension as existing on a continuum rather than being binary. Individuals who see themselves as highly introverted or extraverted are probably on the more extreme end of the continuum. However, many people will be more in the middle of the continuum, seeing themselves as having both elements of introversion and extraversion. Sometimes individuals will combine their types across the four dimensions to report that they are one of 16 personality types (e.g., INTJ, ISFP, ESFJ, ENTP). The potential concern with this approach is that more than one personality type might be seen as equally descriptive, especially if the individual is in the middle of the continuum on one or more dimensions. Therefore, one should be cautious in putting too much weight on the validity of these 16 personality types. Like the Big Five, a safer approach is to compare where partners are on each dimension, noting where they are most similar or different.

One potential problem with the Big Five is that scoring high or low on some dimensions suggests a problem or deficit. For example, low scores on agreeableness indicate the individual is unfriendly, argumentative, competitive, and shows little interest in the needs of others, which is a rather unflattering view of the individual. In contrast, the Myers-Briggs does not portray one type as superior to another. Each type has its own set of strengths and limitations, but one is not better or healthier than the other. Therefore, if you are trying to avoid a deficit view of an individual's behavior by framing it in terms of personality, then this might be easier to accomplish using the Myers-Briggs. If you think of knowledge as constructed rather than being an objective reality, then you have the latitude to choose the framework that you feel offers the most clinical utility for a particular couple rather than use the framework that you believe represents the "objective truth."

Regardless of the framework you choose, the important point is that when couples run into conflict in a relationship, we should consider the possibility that personality may be a contributing factor. Because personality traits are relatively stable, differences in personality can be the basis for many perpetual problems (Chapter 4). When we recognize that personality features are playing a role in the couple's dynamics, then we can help couples learn to accept each other's differences, perhaps even embracing how the differences can bring value to the relationship (Christensen et al., 2015).

In addition, it may be important to frame a partner's behavior in terms of personality rather than as a deficit in caring. For example, Kelly questioned whether Deborah cared about her because she rarely would spend time socializing with her or doing pleasurable activities together.

Instead, Deborah seemed preoccupied with doing chores and errands, or she would be absorbed in a book or gardening. The therapist helped Kelly see that Deborah's behavior was more a reflection of her personality rather than her level of caring for Kelly. While Kelly was high on the extraversion and perceiving end of the continuum, Deborah was high on the introversion and judging side. Being a judger, Deborah felt a great deal of pressure to get chores and other responsibilities done, leading her to often feel overextended. As an introvert, she felt a strong pull to spend some of her time doing solitary activities (e.g., reading, gardening) to recharge her depleted batteries.

It is important to note that differences in personalities do not always cause problems, and they may even be an asset in many ways. Differences in personality may work in complementary ways. For example, Kelly's perceiving side could encourage Deborah to protect more time for play rather than always focusing on getting her work done first. Rather than assume that a couple's differences are problematic, consider the possibility that their differences are complementary and a strength. Conversely, individuals who are similar on a personality dimension may view themselves as being highly compatible. Yet this similarity could be a potential vulnerability in some circumstances. For example, two people who are highly introverted may struggle to make new friends when moving to a new city compared to a couple where one is introverted and the other is extraverted.

Emotional Sensitivities

Several models of therapy note that individuals can bring emotional sensitivities into the relationship that can impact how they relate to their partner. For example, identifying emotional sensitivities is one of the E's in the DEEP analysis that an IBCT therapist will use to conceptualize couples (Christensen et al., 2015). In the Gottman approach, mapping the anatomy of the fight includes identifying emotional sensitivities that may get activated (J. M. Gottman & J. S. Gottman, 2015). As discussed in Chapter 2, conducting individual histories can often uncover the origins of these emotional sensitivities because they typically arise from one's childhood or past relationships.

One of the ways that emotional sensitivities may manifest in the relationship is through low self-esteem. Therefore, it can be helpful to assess if either individual has issues with self-esteem. Individuals with low self-esteem may experience a variety of problems in intimate relationships. For example, individuals can have difficulty with intimacy because they fear their flaws and shortcomings will be exposed. Insecurities due to low self-esteem can also breed anger and jealousy. The ways in which individuals cope with low self-esteem, such as withdrawal or substance use, can also create problems in relationships.

Individuals with low self-esteem have often experienced traumatic events or abuse in their childhood. Children who have experienced some form of abuse may incorrectly internalize a belief that there is something wrong with them to explain why the abuse happened to them. Meredith, for example, suffered severe sexual abuse as a teenager. Meredith erroneously believed that she was partially responsible for the sexual abuse that had occurred to her. Being sexually abused not only negatively impacted her feelings of self-worth, but also made it difficult for her to be sexually intimate with her partner. Having sex with her partner would sometimes trigger feelings of shame that were associated with the sexual abuse. As a result, Meredith frequently did not enjoy sex and was reluctant to initiate any sexual contact with her partner.

In severe cases, individuals with low self-esteem will benefit from a referral for individual therapy to address the underlying causes. If self-esteem issues are a result of some traumatic experiences, then a therapist can help the individual to process these experiences to lessen their impact. For example, seeking out therapy for the sexual abuse helped Meredith in a number of ways. Her therapist was able to help Meredith see that she was not to blame for the sexual abuse she experienced. As her feelings of guilt about the abuse began to subside, Meredith slowly became more comfortable with her own sexuality, which increased her ability to enjoy sex with her partner.

During assessment, be aware that emotional sensitivities can arise in other ways too. For example, individuals who have been hurt by past affairs in previous relationships may have issues of trust. Painful experiences from an individual's family of origin can also be activated by relationship dynamics. Alejandro and Zia came to therapy due to conflict over several issues. However, one of the key issues that would spark conflict for the couple was if Zia did not complete tasks or follow through on something that she promised to do. In addition, she was often late due to poorly organizing her time. When these things would happen, Alejandro would become very upset with Zia. Further assessment uncovered that Zia had undiagnosed ADHD, which was a key reason that she struggled with the behaviors that made Alejandro upset. In addition, the therapist discovered that Alejandro had an emotional sensitivity that was triggered by Zia's ADHD behaviors. During the individual histories, Alejandro disclosed that he had been raised by a mother who had a severe drug addiction. Her drug addiction led Alejandro to experience neglect and a chaotic childhood. Therefore, negative memories of his childhood would be triggered by Zia's ADHD behaviors.

Mental and Physical Illness

Both mental and physical illness can have a significant impact on a couple's relationship, especially if they are of a chronic nature. Therefore, it is important that both be assessed for when evaluating character. For example, recognizing that Zia had undiagnosed ADHD was an important element in the treatment of Alejandro and Zia. It can also be important to assess the impact that either a mental or physical illness can have on the couple's relationship. Because there are strong parallels between the impact of physical and mental illness on relationships, these will be addressed together in this section. Finally, it is important to assess how effectively the couple is managing either mental or physical illness, especially if it is chronic in nature.

Assessing for Mental and Physical Illness

With proper treatment, the negative impact of mental or physical illness on the relationship can often be addressed. However, one first needs to recognize that a mental illness exists before it can be treated. Like the case of Alejandro and Zia, the couple may be unaware that one of them is struggling with an undiagnosed mental or physical illness. Therefore, during assessment you need to be vigilant to any clues that mental or physical illness may be a contributing factor.

If you suspect mental illness, then you should inquire if the individual has been diagnosed with mental illness before. If so, does this appear to be the same mental illness that was diagnosed before, or is it a new diagnosis?

You may want to administer assessment instruments or screening tools to further evaluate if the individual meets the criteria for the mental health diagnosis. For example, if you suspect depression, you might want to administer one of several assessment instruments available to evaluate depression (e.g., PHQ-9, Beck Depression Inventory). In the example of Alejandro and Zia, the therapist administered the Adult ADHD Self-Report Scale (ASRS v1.1) Symptom Checklist (Kessler et al., 2005) to explore whether Zia might have ADHD. In some cases, a referral to a psychiatrist or specialist may need to be made to confirm the diagnosis.

In addition to recognizing if an undiagnosed mental illness exists, you also need to be alert to the possibility that an individual with mental health issues has been misdiagnosed. For example, Xavier was diagnosed with unipolar depression, which was being treated with Zoloft by his primary care physician. However, the medication did not seem to be reducing his depression much, which was negatively impacting the couple's marriage. When evaluating his mental health history, the therapist began to suspect that Xavier may have bipolar disorder rather than unipolar depression. Further assessment seemed to confirm this suspicion, so a referral was made to a psychiatrist to evaluate whether a different medication might be necessary in light of his new diagnosis.

During the individual history, you should ask if either individual has any health issues. If so, you can explore the impact it has had upon the individual, as well as the relationship. Susan disclosed that she had fibromyalgia and described periods where she experienced extreme fatigue. Susan complained that her husband did not understand her illness, and that he would feel rejected whenever she declined his offer to do something together when she was suffering from extreme fatigue. He assumed that she simply did not want to spend time with him rather than recognize that she was struggling with her fibromyalgia.

Although uncovering an undiagnosed mental illness is more commonly encountered in couple therapy, it is also possible that an undiagnosed physical illness may contribute to relationship problems. Dwayne and Rashida came to therapy complaining of conflict in their relationship. Rashida complained that in the last 6 months, Dwayne had become difficult to live with due to his increasing irritability, which often sparked conflict for the couple. Dwayne agreed that he had recently become more irritable for reasons he did not understand, and he also complained of fatigue. The therapist immediately suspected depression, but there did not seem to be an easily discernible precipitating event to cause the depression. The therapist recommended that Dwayne get a physical check-up to rule out any physical cause for the fatigue. Initial blood work by the primary care physician uncovered high calcium levels in the blood, and an eventual diagnosis of hyperparathyroidism. The couple soon learned that Dwayne's irritability and fatigue were symptoms of his hyperparathyroidism. If you suspect a possible underlying medical condition, then making an appropriate referral will be necessary to rule this out.

Ways Mental and Physical Illness Can Impact Relationships

An individual's mental or physical illness can have a significant impact on a couple's relationship. Furthermore, the couple's relationship may have implications for how the mental or physical illness is managed. Recognizing this bidirectional influence has led to the development of couple-based interventions to address a number of mental and physical illnesses (Snyder & Balderrama-Durbin, 2020). The following section describes various ways that mental or physical illness can impact a couple's relationship, which can inform your assessment.

Vicious Cycles

Chapter 4 discussed the importance of assessing for vicious cycles or negative interactional patterns when working with couples. Vicious cycles can emerge around mental and physical illness, which need to be addressed in addition to treating the illness. Consider the following examples.

Tyrene and Jasmine are caught in a vicious cycle around Tyrene's drinking. When Tyrene drinks, Jasmine becomes worried and upset, which she shows by being critical of Tyrene and his drinking. Because Tyrene feels attacked by Jasmine, he retreats into drinking to escape his negative feelings of disappointing both Jasmine and himself. However, drinking to cope with his emotions only perpetuates the cycle.

Amy and Peter argue over Amy's gambling problem. Peter interprets Amy's gambling as a sign that she does not care about him or the marriage. This leads Peter to complain and eventually yell at Amy. This makes Amy very anxious, which only fuels her compulsion to gamble, further perpetuating the cycle.

Change in Roles or Power

You should also assess if mental or physical illness has impacted the roles and power in a couple's relationship. Jose and Margarita are in their late 30s, married with two young children. Jose was a successful businessman, while Margarita was a stay-at-home mother. Jose had an unfortunate auto accident that left him partially paralyzed. During his recovery, Jose became depressed because he was no longer able to provide economically for his family. He was upset because Margarita was forced to go back to work. Jose felt like he had lost his role as head of the household and was now like one of the children needing to be taken care of by Margarita.

Financial Stress

Mental and physical illness can also put a strain on a couple financially. As the example of Jose illustrates, serious mental or physical illness may impact the person's ability to work, which can place a financial hardship on the couple. In addition, expenses related to treating the mental or physical illness may be high, adding to the hardship. For example, some medications to treat mental or physical illness can be expensive. Other medical bills associated with physical illness can also add up, putting individuals into significant financial debt.

Emotional Withdrawal

Mental illness or physical illness can lead individuals to emotionally withdraw, which can create problems in an intimate relationship. For example, when Chantelle would become depressed, she would isolate and withdraw from her partner Sandy. Sandy's attempts to engage her partner were unsuccessful, leading Sandy to feel rejected and lonely in the relationship. Chantelle was aware of Sandy's unhappiness, which only added to her depression because she believed she was a bad partner and that Sandy deserved better. Individuals with physical illness can also emotionally withdraw as they cope with their illness. Mikeal suffered from intense, chronic back pain. On the days in which the pain was most severe, he would focus on his pain and emotionally shut down.

Irritability

A common symptom associated with mental health disorders can be irritability. For example, irritability is commonly associated with depression, particularly among men. Individuals who struggle with chronic pain or other mental disorders (e.g., bipolar, anxiety) may also experience irritability. Regardless of its source, irritability has the potential to trigger conflict in the relationship. This was true for Larry and Melissa. Larry suffered from chronic back pain due to a war injury. Larry and Melissa had successfully resolved many of the marital issues through therapy when Larry had surgery for this back pain. When the couple returned to therapy after the surgery, Larry remarked that his marriage had improved as a result of the surgery. When asked to explain why, he said that the couple seemed to be bickering less. He attributed this change to the fact that he no longer felt back pain, which made him chronically irritable and prone to making negative remarks to his wife.

Reduction in Pleasurable Activities

Physical and mental illness can also prevent individuals from doing pleasurable activities that can promote connection with their partner (see Chapter 7 on caring). For example, depressed individuals may stop doing pleasurable activities because they experience less pleasure out of them and a lack motivation to do things. Chronic pain or fatigue can also prevent individuals from doing pleasurable activities. Alexander used to be very athletic. However, due to nerve pain in his legs and feet, even going on short walks like he and his wife used to enjoy doing was painful and something he avoided.

Impact on Sexual Intimacy

You should also assess the impact that mental or physical illness can have upon a couple's sex life (see Chapter 8). Mental and physical illness can impact sex in a host of ways. Depression may cause low sexual desire or cardiovascular disease can create erectile difficulties. Diabetes also interferes with sexual functioning in a number of ways, such as reducing desire, arousal, or the ability to have an orgasm. Dolores had frequent vaginal infections due to her diabetes, which led her to avoid sex because intercourse was painful. Chronic pain can also reduce a couple's ability to enjoy sex. Laura was a 50-year-old woman who suffered from severe, chronic back pain. Two surgeries were unsuccessful in resolving her pain. Laura was unable to tolerate sexual intercourse with her partner due to her back pain, which had previously been an important way in which she and her partner had connected. Medications to treat mental or physical illness also can impact sexual functioning as a side effect. For example, antidepressants like Paxil, Prozac, or Zoloft can reduce sexual desire in individuals.

Suicide

When dealing with mental or physical illness, it is important that you be vigilant for the possibility of suicide. For example, relationship distress can be a trigger for individuals with mental illness to contemplate or attempt suicide. Don't hesitate to ask clients if they have had any thoughts of harming or killing themselves, as well if they have plans and means to kill themselves. In determining the level of risk, it can be helpful to know whether the individual has a history of past attempts. Therefore, it is recommended that you inquire about this when doing the individual histories (see Chapter 2). It is also important to explore if the partner has concerns about their partner's safety, and how these concerns are managed.

Managing Mental and Physical Illness

You should also assess how the couple is attempting to cope with the mental or physical illness, especially if it is chronic in nature. This will help you determine if there are ways in which the couple can improve how they manage the mental or physical illness in order to reduce its impact on the relationship.

Assessment of Treatment

You should assess if the individual has sought treatment for the mental or physical disorder. For example, is the individual currently being treated? If so, how effective is the treatment? If the individual is not seeking treatment, what is the reason why? In some cases, finances may be a barrier to seeking proper treatment. For some, the stigma attached to mental health issues may prevent them from seeking out treatment (e.g., therapy, medication). However, getting proper treatment can make a huge difference. When Evan and Alexandria came to therapy, they reported significant conflict in the relationship. Evan would alternate between being very depressed and being very irritable. Upon further assessment, Evan was diagnosed with bipolar disorder. Once Evan was stabilized on medication, the couple reported that conflict in their relationship was reduced by 50–70%.

Assess Understanding of the Illness

It is also important to assess both partner's understanding of the mental or physical illness. Do both have a proper understanding of the illness, or do they have some misconceptions or lack of knowledge about it? Some individuals may not be aware that some of their problems are symptoms of the illness. As a result, they may misattribute their problems to bad character traits. For example, many individuals with undiagnosed ADHD have grown up believing they are stupid or lazy. With proper education, they begin to appreciate how ADHD has contributed to their struggles.

It is equally important to assess the partner's understanding of the mate's illness. In the earlier example, Peter assumed that Amy's gambling was a rational choice she made. He did not recognize the compulsive nature of gambling that Amy experienced. Therefore, Peter was hurt and angry every time she gambled because he thought that she was essentially choosing gambling over him.

Assessment of Self-Care

Dealing with a physical or mental illness can be stressful. Therefore, it is important that you assess if individuals are practicing good self-care.

Self-care can take on many forms, such as seeking support from others, eating properly, getting plenty of rest, or protecting time in one's schedule for pleasurable activities to recharge. Sean and his wife Gerri came to therapy to address conflict in their marriage. Sean was diagnosed with bipolar disorder, which did not seem to be well managed. During assessment, the therapist learned that Sean drank large amounts of Coca Cola each day. Because of the large amount of caffeine he was consuming daily, Sean often had difficulty going to sleep. As a result, many nights he would stay up into the early morning hours working on his computer. Once Sean significantly scaled back on the amount of Coca Cola that he drank, he was able to be more consistent in going to bed at a reasonable hour, which helped to reduce his bipolar symptoms.

Living with a person who has a mental or physical illness can be stressful for partners too, especially if they are a caregiver in some capacity. Therefore, you also need to assess if partners are practicing good self-care. If partners do not exercise good self-care, anger and resentment is more likely to build up as they experience burnout from their mate's illness. When Angelica and Ernesto came into therapy, Angelica was exhausted. She devoted much of her energy to taking care of Ernesto and his medical needs. She drove him to all his appointments, monitored his medications, and prepared separate meals to accommodate his special dietary needs. Friction had increased in the relationship in the past few months, in part because Angelica was becoming exhausted and resentful of her caregiving duties. She felt like she had no life of her own and that everything revolved around Ernesto's needs. The therapist first reassured Angelica that her feelings and challenges were normal for those in a caregiving role like hers. However, the therapist suggested that she needed to do a better job of protecting some time to address her own needs. Angelica responded by saying that she felt guilty spending time away from her husband, particularly because he was so dependent upon her. The therapist noted that Angelica was in a marathon, but she was running the race at a sprinter's pace. He speculated that she would not be able to sustain this indefinitely, and that she would likely drop out of the race if she continued at this pace. He added that this would have unfortunate consequences not only for her husband, but it would also create a great sense of guilt for her. Practicing better self-care would allow her to stay in the race and reduce resentment, which would better serve both her and her husband's needs.

Social Support

Assessing a couple's level of social support is another important consideration. A social support system can potentially help in many ways, including providing emotional support, spiritual support, education, or instrumental support (e.g., provide respite care for a caregiver). Therefore, it can be important to assess what needs each partner may have, and whether they have individuals in their social support network who can help meet these needs. At the therapist's urging, Angelica eventually joined a caregiver's support group, which both normalized some of her challenges and provided connection to others, thereby reducing her sense of isolation.

Separate the Person From the Illness

Finally, it can be important to assess the extent to which individuals and their partners define the person by their illness. It is important to recognize that individuals are not completely defined by their illness. Individuals do not go around telling others, "I am a cold." Rather, they say, "I have a cold." In the case of the cold, the individuals have an illness, but they are not the illness. Individuals often make this distinction when discussing a person's physical illness, but they may not do so if the person is struggling with a mental illness. Unfortunately, it is all too easy to slip into saying, "He is a schizophrenic," rather than saying, "He has schizophrenia." Saying that someone is schizophrenic, bipolar, or borderline overlooks the fact that the person is much more than their illness. It overshadows a person's other positive qualities.

Sometimes individuals and their partners need help seeing the person as separate from their illness. One way that therapists can do this is to externalize the disorder consistent with a narrative perspective (White & Epston, 1990). When Sean and his wife Gerri came to therapy, it was apparent that the bipolar disorder with which Sean had recently been diagnosed was significantly impacting the couple's marriage. The couple would often have arguments, particularly on days when Sean struggled with his mood due to his bipolar disorder. Sean told the therapist, "I am bipolar" in a resigned tone that suggested that he had been given a death sentence. The therapist wanted to help both Sean and Gerri see that Sean was more than just his bipolar disorder. Underneath the illness was a man who was bright and insightful, as well as kind and caring. Because the couple had told the therapist that they had a large stuffed bear in their living room, he suggested to the couple that Sean's bipolar disorder was like a big bear that was living with the couple. The therapist told Sean he could use his strengths to help combat the bear. In addition, Gerri was encouraged to see the bear or bipolar disorder as the enemy, and not Sean. If the couple could work together, then they could fight the bear together rather than each other. For example, Sean was instructed to tell Gerri that the bear was out if he recognized that his bipolar symptoms were bothering him on that particular day. This helped Gerri take his irritability less personally, and she tried to be supportive by asking him what she could do to help him fight the bear.

Assessing Strengths

Much of this chapter has focused on assessing how character features might negatively impact a couple's relationship. However, when assessing character features, it is important to uncover strengths and not just problems or concerns. When assessing for strengths, you can take a variety of strategies.

First, you can ask directly about strengths. For example, you can ask each person what they see as their partner's strengths. This can be asked in a variety of ways, such as asking what they like about their partner. What first attracted them to their partner? What do they admire in their partner?

Second, you can look for strengths that are evident outside the relationship. The therapist working with Nathaniel was encouraging him to be more assertive in stating his needs to his wife. The therapist noted that in his role as a nurse, he was able to be appropriately assertive with patients when necessary. The therapist explored how his ability to be assertive at work could help him be more assertive at home.

Third, it is important that a character feature can be both an asset and a liability. An individual who is stubborn in terms of temperament can also be viewed as persistent, which can be a desirable trait in some circumstances. Carter and Ben both struggled with chronic mental illness. Although each person's mental illness sometimes placed a strain on the couple's relationship, they could also each empathize with the other person's struggles because they too had personal experience with mental illness.

Conclusion

The personal qualities that individuals bring into the relationship are important to consider in a couple's assessment (see Table 10.1). Similarities and differences in personality between the partners have the potential to impact the relationship. For example, differences in personality have the potential to be strengths by being complementary in nature or the basis for attraction. However, they can also be the source of perpetual problems that create conflict. It is also important to assess for any emotional sensitivities that individuals bring into the relationship from their childhood or past relationships. These emotional sensitivities can make individuals more reactive to certain issues. Mental illness or physical illness can be another important consideration, particularly given the number of ways they can negatively impact a couple's relationship. Beyond assessing the impact of mental or physical illness on a couple, it is also important to evaluate how well the couple is managing it. Throughout our assessment of character, we should also be vigilant to ask about and look for strengths.

Table 10.1 Assessing Character Features

The following questions can assist you in assessing the extent to which character features are strengths or areas of concern:
1. What is the personality profile for each person (e.g., Big Five, Myers-Briggs)?
2. In what ways do personality differences create problems (e.g., perpetual problems, personality attributes are seen as deficits)? In what ways are they a strength (e.g., differences are complementary in nature)?
3. What emotional sensitivities do partners bring into the relationship? What is the origin of these sensitivities?

(Continued)

Table 10.1 (Continued)

4. Is there evidence that physical or mental illness is impacting one or both partners?

5. What is the impact of the physical or mental illness upon the relationship? Is the couple engaged in a vicious cycle around the mental or physical illness? How does the mental or physical illness impact the couple's connection (e.g., emotional withdrawal, reduction of pleasurable activities, sex)? Does it impact the couple's relationship in other ways (e.g., finances, power/roles)?

6. Is there any threat of self-harm or suicide?

7. Do both individuals have a good understanding of the illness? Would either benefit from more psychoeducation?

8. Is the individual getting proper treatment for the illness? If not, what barriers are keeping them from seeking treatment (e.g., finances, stigma)?

9. Is the couple practicing good self-care?

10. Does the couple have good social support?

11. Are both able to separate the illness from the person?

12. What are the strengths of each individual in the relationship?

11

CHILDREN
An Eighth C?

The 7 Cs discussed so far are applicable to all couples. Although not all couples have children, many do. Children can have a huge influence on relationships. In some cases, issues around parenting may be the major source of conflict. The demands of taking care of children may also impact how much time and energy a couple has to devote to their relationship. Therefore, it seems appropriate to add children as an eighth C to the framework when assessing couples who are also parents.

General Assessment Considerations

When assessing the impact of children on a couple's relationship, a number of factors can be assessed. You should first establish whether or not the couple has any children. This includes biological or adoptive children, as well as stepchildren. In some cases, the couple may be raising grandchildren or other extended family relatives.

DOI: 10.4324/9781003161967-11

If the couple has children, then it can be helpful to collect some basic information about the children. For example, what are the ages of the children? This can help you understand where the couple or family are at in the developmental life cycle. You should also inquire which children, if any, live in the home. In addition, you also need to learn if any of the children have special needs.

Answering these questions can help you formulate some hypotheses about the potential impact of children on the couple's relationship, particularly in terms of the couple's ability to protect time for the relationship. For example, the time and energy required to raise two children under the age of 5 is likely more than that required for two children in their late teens. In addition, younger children will require childcare if the parents spend time away from home, which can present an obstacle for some parents. As a result, parents with younger children may face more challenges in protecting time for their relationship. Protecting time and energy for the relationship will be even more difficult if one or more of the children have special needs.

In some cases, deciding on the number of children to have is a source of conflict. Some couples may already have children but disagree on whether to have additional children. For example, Eduardo and Felicia already had three children. Although Felicia strongly desired to have a fourth child, Eduardo was content with three children and worried about the couple's financial ability to have a fourth child. The case of Britney and Craig that was described in Chapter 9 (contract) illustrates how some couples may disagree on whether to be parents at all.

Some couples agree on their desire to become parents, but they may disagree on the timing of when to start a family. Spenser wanted to be more established in his career and financially secure before having children, whereas Gretchen was eager to become a parent as soon as possible. She also feared that delaying having children would make it more difficult for her to get pregnant.

Infertility can create a number of challenges or stressors for couples (Shreffler et al., 2020), which may lead some couples to seek out therapy. For example, couples may struggle on knowing how to best support one another with infertility. It is also not uncommon for couples to experience challenges in their sexual relationship due to infertility. Couples can also disagree on how much of their financial and emotional resources to invest in fertility treatments in an effort to conceive. A detailed discussion of infertility is beyond the scope of this chapter, but Shreffler and her colleagues (2020) provide an overview of what should be included in a psychosocial assessment when couples seek help with infertility.

For couples with children, you should assess if they are experiencing any conflict over differences in parenting. For example, conflict can arise if one parent perceives that the other parent is not taking an active enough role in parenting. Natasha complained that Desmond was overly preoccupied with his work and was not spending enough time with her and the kids. Desmond protested that his job was important because it provided financially for the family. As the case of Natasha and Desmond illustrates, sometimes gender issues can play a role in this dynamic. Desmond assumed that his primary role was to be the economic provider for his family while his wife Natasha would be the primary caretaker of the children. It can be helpful to determine in cases like this where individuals learned messages about what it means to be a father or a mother (e.g., family of origin, society) and to examine the potential validity or limitations of those messages.

Differences in parenting styles, especially around discipline, can also create conflict. Charlene accused Karen of being overly lenient as a parent. She complained that Karen seldom set appropriate limits with their children, and that she would frequently spoil and indulge them. This issue created a constant source of friction in the couple's relationship.

Like other issues, negative interactional patterns can emerge around parenting issues. Therefore, it is important to assess for possible vicious cycles around parenting (see Chapter 4 on conflict resolution). For example, Charlene and Karen became polarized over the issue of disciplining the children. Karen became even more lenient in response to what she perceived as Charlene being overly strict with the children. However, Charlene felt like she had to be stricter with regard to discipline to compensate for Karen's leniency.

Finally, it can be important to consider the impact of the couple's relationship upon the children. For example, to what extent are the children exposed to conflict between the couple, and what impact does it have upon them? Have the children been exposed to any domestic violence? Are the children triangulated into the couple's conflict in any way? In some cases, you may need to address with the couple how their conflict is having a negative impact upon the children.

Couple Relationships and Stepfamilies

The impact of children on relationships can be even more pronounced if one or both partners have children from previous relationships. For many couples, this can put an additional strain on a new relationship for several reasons, which should be assessed for when working with couples in stepfamilies. This section focuses primarily on the couple's relationship within a stepfamily, but a number of other clinical considerations are also necessary when thinking about the overall needs of the stepfamily system.

As previously noted, taking care of children's needs can detract from the time the couple has to devote to nurturing their own relationship. This can be a significant challenge for new couples where one or both already have children (Brimhall, 2020; Michaels, 2011). Couples in stepfamilies will ideally want to dedicate time to building and nurturing their new relationship, yet they must also remain attentive to the needs of the children. Therefore, it is important to assess if the couple has been able to strike a proper balance between these competing needs (Brimhall, 2020; Papernow, 2015). Devoting too much time or attention to one or the other can create problems. If a parent devotes too much attention to the needs of their children, the new mate may feel marginalized or neglected, which will create conflict in the relationship. However, if a parent focuses too much attention on the new mate, then the children will feel threatened by the new relationship. The children will likely express jealousy of the stepparent and see them as an unwelcome intruder into their family. Protecting one-on-one time for the various subsystems (couple, parent-child, stepparent-child) can help address this challenge (Brimhall, 2020; Papernow, 2015).

You should also assess if the couple has developed an appropriate plan for integrating the stepparent into the parenting role (Brimhall, 2020; Michaels, 2011; Papernow, 2015). It is important the stepparent first establish a relationship with the children before assuming a disciplinary role, which Papernow (2015) refers to as "connection before correction." A common mistake that couples make is to prematurely put the stepparent into a disciplinary role. For example, Nari brought her two sons (12 and 14) into her new marriage with Kellen. Kellen was a military veteran who highly prized discipline and a respect for authority, and he worked hard to instill these values into his two sons (15 and 18) from his first marriage. In contrast, Nari had a rather nonconfrontational style, which extended to her parenting. Kellen believed that Nari was too lax with her two sons and resolved to get her sons into shape. However, Nari felt that Kellen was overly harsh and strict with her sons, which created tension in the couple's new relationship. Furthermore, Nari's two children resented Kellen's attempts to parent them, which created further tension and conflict in the family. The ability to step into a parenting role as a stepparent may depend upon the age of the children, which is typically easier with younger children (Brimhall, 2020; Michaels, 2011; Papernow, 2015). In contrast, older children may be resistant to a stepparent assuming a parental role with them.

Individuals with children from previous relationships may still have contact with former partners or spouses with whom they are still co-parenting the children (Michaels, 2011; Papernow, 2015). Unfortunately, these relationships can be contentious. Therefore, you should assess to what extent the couple has created a working co-parenting relationship with the nonresidential parent. Issues in this area also can trigger loyalty issues for the children (Brimhall, 2020). If a stepparent is critical of the nonresidential parent, the child may become angry at the stepparent due to their loyalty to their parent, which only complicates the stepparent's efforts to form a positive bond with the child.

You should also assess if financial issues related to being in a stepfamily are present. Child support can be one source of contention. Violet complained about the child support that Wyatt was paying for his two children from a previous marriage. Although she wanted to support Wyatt being a good father to his children, the amount of the child support was impacting the couple's standard of living. She also expressed resentment that most of the burden of paying child support fell to her because she made considerably more money than Wyatt. Conflict around finances in a stepfamily can also emerge if a mate shows preferential treatment in how they spend or allocate money. For example, Nari complained that Kellen would spend considerably more money on buying birthday and Christmas gifts for his own sons in comparison to his stepsons. Conflict can also emerge around wills, particularly if there is disagreement around how much money should be given to the current mate versus the children from previous relationships.

Conclusion

For some couples, children could be added as an eighth C to the framework to ensure that the impact of children on the relationship has been properly considered. For example, disagreements over the number of desired children, parental involvement, or disciplinary styles can negatively impact a relationship. Devoting too much attention to the needs of the children at the expense of the relationship can also erode relationship quality. Couples who bring children from previous relationships not only face these challenges, but other ones as well (e.g., developing an appropriate parental plan for involving the stepparent, creating an effective co-parenting relationship with previous mates, issues around finances). Table 11.1 summarizes some of the important questions that should be considered when working with couples with children.

Table 11.1 Assessment Questions Regarding Children

The following questions can assist you in assessing the role of children in the couple's relationship:

1. Does the couple care for any children (e.g., biological, adoption, stepparent, grandchildren)?
2. What are the ages of the children? Which children live at home? Do any of the children have special needs?
3. To what extent do children impact the couple's ability to protect time for their relationship?
4. Does the couple agree on the number of children they want, as well as the timing of building their family?
5. Is the couple impacted by infertility?
6. Are there any issues or disagreements over the level of parental involvement?
7. Are there any issues or disagreements over differences in parenting styles (e.g., discipline)?
8. What is the impact of the couple's conflict upon the children?

The following questions can assist you in assessing some of the special challenges that couples who bring children from previous relationships may face:

1. Does the couple have a proper balance between focusing on the needs of their relationship and those of the children?

2. Has the couple developed an appropriate parental plan (e.g., connection before correction)?

3. Has the couple been able to establish an effective co-parenting relationship with ex-partners?

4. Does the couple experience any issues around finances related to being in a stepfamily (e.g., conflict over child support, showing favoritism)?

12

MOVING BEYOND THE INITIAL ASSESSMENT

This chapter will discuss how to translate the information you have collected through assessment into a treatment plan, including how to use the Cs to provide feedback to a couple. We will also explore how you will need to continue with assessment even as you move into the treatment phase. For example, you will need to assess how the couple is responding to treatment and when they are ready for termination. Therefore, assessment is an ongoing process that extends beyond the initial phase of therapy.

Developing a Treatment Plan

Do You Take an Integrative Approach?

Through your assessment, you have collected a wealth of information about a couple at this point. The challenge you now face is how to develop an effective treatment plan that will guide your work with the couple.

DOI: 10.4324/9781003161967-12

One of the questions you will need to confront is whether to select an existing model of couple therapy (e.g., IBCT, EFT, Gottman approach) to guide treatment, or take a more integrative approach. Rather than viewing this as a dichotomous choice, you can think of your choices as existing on a continuum. On one end of the continuum, you could choose to be a purist in following an established model. On the opposite end of the spectrum, you could take a highly integrative approach that draws upon material from multiple models. Using the 7 Cs framework offers one potential way of integrating ideas from various models, although other models also exist (e.g., Integrative Systemic Therapy). In between are different shades of integration. For example, a low level of integration might mean that you incorporate only one or two ideas or interventions from another model into an existing model, but you remain largely true to the primary model.

There are both advantages and disadvantages to being either a purist or using an integrative approach. One advantage to being a purist is that the blueprint for using the model has already been laid out. For example, EFT lays out a nine-step process for addressing couple distress (Johnson, 2015). Thus, relying on an established model may provide you greater guidance on how to implement treatment, which may be comforting to therapists who are relatively new to seeing couples. In contrast, you will need to rely more on your clinical expertise and intuition on how to incorporate ideas from different models or plan treatment when using an integrative approach. Therefore, therapists with more clinical experience may be more confident in using an integrative approach.

The primary advantage of using an integrative approach is that you may be able to better tailor your approach to the couple's needs (Kelly et al., 2019; Lebow, 2019; Snyder & Balderrama-Durbin, 2012). A particular model may be well suited to address some of the issues or needs of a couple but not others. Integrating elements from other models or sources may allow you to address the issues that are not emphasized in a particular model. Thus, being integrative may allow you to be more comprehensive and flexible in how you approach the couple's issues.

If you integrate concepts into an evidence-based model, then you need to be aware that it could potentially impact the effectiveness of the primary model. The models emphasized in this book have strong empirical support. For example, EFT (Wiebe & Johnson, 2016), IBCT (Roddy et al., 2016), and PREP (Tonelli et al., 2016) have been proven to be effective through randomized clinical trials, the gold standard for evaluating the effectiveness of treatments. Elements of the Gottman approach have also been incorporated into various programs (e.g., Art and Science of Love, Bringing Baby Home, Loving Couples Loving Children) that have been evaluated using randomized clinical trials and found to be effective (J. S. Gottman & J. M. Gottman, 2015). Using models evaluated through clinical trials gives you greater confidence in their effectiveness.

However, the more you integrate material from other sources into an established model, the more the treatment approach will deviate from the version of the model that was proven to be effective through research. Although integrating concepts from other models could enhance the effectiveness of the model, it could also potentially make it less effective (Snyder & Balderrama-Durbin, 2012). Therefore, it is uncertain whether a more integrative model will perform the same, better, or worse than the original model upon which it is based. One way to address this concern is to continually assess the effectiveness of your treatment, which is addressed later in the chapter.

Different Approaches to Integration

If you decide to integrate material from other models or sources, then there are different ways to do this. The first approach is to integrate psychoeducation from other sources to reinforce or expand upon the existing theoretical concepts or interventions within a model. For example, a therapist using IBCT could introduce the couple to the 5 Love Languages (Chapman, 2010) when encouraging a couple to increase the demonstration of caring behaviors. Providing psychoeducation on the 5 Love Languages could encourage the individuals to choose caring behaviors that are consistent with their partner's preferred love languages.

A second approach is to remain conceptually true to one model, but you integrate interventions from other models that are consistent with the primary model. For example, a therapist might use interventions like heightening or empathic conjectures from EFT to facilitate the expression of softer emotions within the IBCT model.

The third approach is to integrate theoretical concepts from other sources (e.g., different theoretical models) into an existing model. This allows you to expand the model to address issues or needs that may not be adequately addressed by just one model (Kelly et al., 2019; Lebow, 2019; Snyder & Balderrama-Durbin, 2012). For example, a therapist might primarily use a DBT approach (Fruzzetti & Payne, 2015) with a couple because one or both have difficulties with emotional dysregulation. However, the therapist might want to integrate elements of EFT into the work, such as understanding and reframing each person's behavior from an attachment perspective. A discussion of how to integrate theoretical concepts across models is beyond the scope of this book. However, Lebow (2019) describes various traditions that have been followed to accomplish this. These include creating an overarching or meta-framework for integrating concepts across models, developing algorithms to guide treatment with less of an emphasis on theoretical integration, looking at common factors across models, and identifying underlying principles to doing effective therapy.

As you integrate elements from other models, you also need to be aware that it may impact how the primary model is delivered. For example, EFT is a highly experiential way of doing couple therapy. Introducing skills or psychoeducation from other models could alter the experiential nature of the approach. As noted, you need to be mindful of how this could potentially alter the effectiveness of the approach.

Factors to Weigh in Choosing a Particular Model

If you decide to base your treatment primarily or exclusively on one approach, how do you choose which model? There are multiple considerations which might inform your decision. These include the following:

Is there empirical support for the model? This book has emphasized concepts from models with empirical support (e.g., EFT, Gottman approach, IBCT, PREP). We can have more confidence in our work if we use or draw upon models that are backed by research. Therefore, you should give serious consideration to using models that have empirical evidence supporting them (J. S. Gottman & J. M. Gottman, 2015; Kelly et al., 2019).

Which model is the best in terms of addressing the couple's issues? Although many of the models are versatile in terms of addressing various couple issues, you may find that one model may be a better fit than others in addressing a couple's issues. For example, I have found that EFT is a good fit when one or both individuals question their partner's love for them. Often this points to unmet attachment needs, which EFT targets. However, EFT is more difficult to apply if the couple has differences that create conflict that don't necessarily lead them to question their love for one another. In these situations, models that incorporate acceptance into the model (e.g., IBCT, DBT, Gottman approach) might be a better fit. If a couple has significant challenges with emotional dysregulation, then DBT should be considered as an option.

Which model is a better fit with the couple's learning style? Models can vary to the extent to which they are experiential or didactic in nature. For example, EFT is a highly experiential approach to therapy, which does not rely on teaching couples skills or offering psychoeducation. In contrast, an approach like PREP focuses on teaching couples skills and providing psychoeducation. Although some couples will find learning skills appealing, it also requires that a couple invest time and effort to practice the skills. Therefore, you should assess if a couple has the motivation to learn the skills. If not, then a more experiential model like EFT might be a better fit.

Which model is a better fit with the therapist's style? Therapists might also have personal preferences for certain models, which could be factored into deciding which model to use. Therapists who use an EFT approach need to be highly comfortable working with emotions. A therapist with an emotion-dismissing meta-emotional style might be uncomfortable working with emotions, especially intense emotions. As a result, EFT would likely not be the best fit for this type of therapist. Instead, the therapist might prefer models where providing psychoeducation and skills development are an integral part of the approach.

If practicing in an agency setting, how does this context inform your decision? Many therapists, particularly early in their career, work in an agency setting. In some settings, a particular model may be emphasized or encouraged. For example, IBCT was emphasized as an approach when working with couples in the VA setting where I worked. Even if a particular model is not emphasized within an agency, your supervisor may have a significant influence on which model you learn and use, especially if you are a beginning therapist. For example, if your supervisor is a certified Gottman or EFT therapist, then your supervisor is likely to offer you feedback from that perspective.

Providing Your Couple Feedback

Prior to beginning treatment, you will want to provide the couple feedback on what you have learned about them through assessment. One way to organize your feedback is to use the 7 Cs (or 8 Cs if children are a salient issue). Couples seem to appreciate receiving feedback using the Cs for at least two reasons. First, the Cs provide feedback in a way that is understandable to the couple. Couples seem to easily grasp the concept of each C after they are briefly described. Second, the couple feels that they are obtaining a thorough assessment of their relationship if the therapist provides feedback in each of the Cs. Couples generally appreciate the thoroughness of the feedback, especially if they have invested multiple sessions on assessment.

Table 12.1 shows an example of what feedback using the 7 Cs looked like for an interracial couple, Andrew and Kiara. The couple came into therapy looking to enhance their relationship by addressing a number of concerns.

Table 12.1 Example of Feedback Using the 7 Cs

The following is illustrative of the feedback that a couple received after assessment using the 7 Cs framework:

Communication and *Conflict Resolution*

- The couple demonstrates rigorous honesty with each other, which both appreciate.
- Communication can sometimes shut down over difficult issues.
- The couple can get caught in a pursue-withdraw cycle at times, especially when Andrew becomes depressed and emotionally withdraws.

Culture

- The couple does not report any challenges in terms of cultural differences arising from being an interracial couple.
- The couple reports that both families are accepting of the couple's interracial relationship. However, the couple notes that Kiara's side of the family is pressuring the couple to get married and have children.
- The couple has an egalitarian relationship.

Commitment

- Both express high commitment to the relationship.

(Continued)

Table 12.1 (Continued)

Caring

- Both trust each other.
- Both report a strong emotional connection to one another.
- In terms of the 5 Love Languages, Kiara's love language appears to be acts of service and Andrew's appears to be physical touch.
- The couple reports some concerns around sexual intimacy (e.g., low sexual desire for Kiara due to sexual trauma).
- Both have tried to be very supportive of each other's personal challenges (e.g., Kiara's sobriety, Andrew's depression).

Contract

- Overall, the couple has established a good contract.
- The couple has some differing expectations on when to get married.
- The couple is in agreement that they do not want to have children in the future.

Character

- Andrew struggles with depression, anxiety, and occasional feelings of unworthiness.
- Kiara is in the early stages of substance use (alcohol) recovery.
- Both Andrew and Kiara are insightful individuals.
- Both Andrew and Kiara are willing to look at themselves and how they might change.

When using the Cs to provide feedback, you should keep a few factors in mind. First, you may note that some issues may significantly overlap with more than one C. For example, Andrew and Kiara were in agreement that they did not want to become parents. Does this belong under contract, or does it belong under the eighth C, children? In a situation like this, you have the option to decide if you want to punctuate it under one C or another. In the example of Andrew and Kiara, the therapist decided to list it under contract, but it could have just as easily been put under children. In situations like this, the important thing is that the issue or strength is identified, not which C it is listed under. However, if more than one C seems appropriate, you also need to consider the possibility that there are two independent factors that strongly influence each other. For example, Andrew's depression contributed to the couple's pursue-withdraw dynamic. In the feedback, the therapist noted both the pursue-withdraw cycle (conflict resolution) and depression (character) as issues needing attention. In this situation, the therapist felt it was appropriate to punctuate them as separate but connected issues, possibly needing to develop separate interventions to target both issues.

Second, it is important to include strengths in the formulation, and not simply focus on areas of concern. It is easy to adopt a deficit perspective on a distressed relationship, especially when the couple has this perspective. However, your job is like a house inspector when providing feedback. You are going to help the couple see where their relationship is sound, as well as areas where problems exist. As you evaluate the couple in each of the Cs, you will ideally ask yourself, "If this C does not seem to be an issue for this particular couple, what are the strengths evident in this area?" In other words, the absence of problems could be an indicator of possible strengths. Even if there are concerns in a particular area, there are also likely strengths that can be identified to help counterbalance the concerns. So, as much as possible, try to identify at least one strength within each C.

Third, the goal of the feedback is to provide new insights for the couple rather than simply provide a recitation of their concerns. To offer new insights, you can ask yourself a number of questions. Have you offered the couple any new concepts for understanding their relationship? For example, the therapist described the 5 Love Languages (Chapman, 2010) to Andrew and Kiara, which was a new concept to both of them. Have you offered the couple a better understanding as to why their problems exist? In the case of Andrew and Kiara, the therapist observed that Kiara's low sexual desire appeared to be linked to her past sexual trauma and sex being painful at times. These connections challenged Andrew's belief that Kiara's lower sexual drive was simply due to her finding him less sexually attractive. Furthermore, the therapist helped Kiara understand that because Andrew had physical touch as one of his love languages, the reduced amount of sex had a significant impact on how loved he felt by Kiara. Have you provided insight into how the couple interacts around the issue, such as potential vicious cycles? The therapist for Andrew and Kiara helped the couple recognize the pursue-withdraw dynamic that would sometimes get activated for the couple, especially when Andrew would emotionally withdraw when depressed. Have you helped the couple identify how contextual factors are influencing the relationship? For example, the therapist explored how Kiara's cultural background appeared to be a factor as to why the couple felt pressure from his family to get married and have children. Have you helped the couple identify where the couple has strengths? Although some couples can easily identify their strengths, some couples struggle to do so. Thankfully, the therapist working with Andrew and Kiara was able to note several strengths the couple possessed, some which were not immediately evident to the couple.

Fourth, couples should be able to see the connection between the feedback and the goals for therapy. Grounding the treatment goals in the feedback gained from assessment will give the couple confidence that the goals are appropriate. Getting the couple's agreement on the goals for therapy is important to get buy in as you move forward in therapy. Otherwise, you may encounter resistance. Although rare, it is possible that the therapist and couple might reach an impasse in terms of agreeing on treatment goals. If this happens, the therapist should refer the couple to another therapist for a second opinion.

It should be noted that conducting an assessment using the Cs does not require that you use the 7 Cs to organize your feedback to the couple. You can choose an alternative way to structure feedback if it provides a better fit with the approach you plan to use. For example, you might decide that IBCT would be the treatment of choice for a particular couple based on the information you collected through assessment. Therefore, you might provide the feedback in a manner more consistent with the IBCT model, such as articulating the couple's theme and providing a DEEP analysis (Christensen et al., 2015).

Regardless of your approach, it is important to assess if the feedback and treatment goals you present resonate with the couple. The couple should be given the opportunity to refine or disagree with the feedback, including the treatment goals. The couple's reaction to the feedback can provide further assessment data, which may be helpful in enhancing or reformulating your understanding of the couple.

Assessment During Treatment

Assessing Progress in Therapy

Assessment does not end after providing feedback and a treatment plan (Balderrama-Durbin et al., 2020). You should continue to assess how the couple is responding to treatment. Is the couple responding well to treatment, making gains? Or does the couple appear to be stuck, perhaps even regressing?

A supervisor early in my career (T. Nelson, personal communication, n.d.) told me that "assessment is intervention, and intervention is assessment." The second part of this axiom is particularly salient during treatment. A couple's response to your interventions can provide important information about a couple. Ideally, a couple's positive response to your interventions will reassure you that your approach is on target. However, it can also be diagnostic if a couple does not respond well to an intervention. For example, a couple's reluctance to do a homework assignment may uncover potential negative consequences to change that had not been evident before. A couple's unwillingness to do an exercise like sensate focus to improve sexual functioning might also uncover a higher level of anxiety about sex than the clinician initially suspected. In some cases, reluctance to do the assignments may reflect that the therapist's approach is not resonating with the couple and may need to be reconsidered.

Clinicians can use different strategies to assess the overall progress that clients are making in therapy. In one approach, the therapist may periodically ask the couple if they are seeing improvement in the relationship. They may supplement this assessment by observing how the couple behaves in session. For example, do they seem less reactive to one another? Is the mood lighter compared to previous sessions, or is the couple more affectionate with one another?

A second approach is to use assessment instruments to measure progress in therapy. For example, a therapist might periodically administer the Dyadic Adjustment Scale (Spanier, 1976) or some other measure of relationship quality to see if the scores are improving over time. A weekly assessment of the couple's progress can also be incorporated into therapy. In the IBCT approach, a Weekly Questionnaire (Christensen et al., 2015) is given to the couple prior to the beginning of each session. The Weekly Questionnaire provides the therapist several pieces of information, including a snapshot of how the couple is feeling about the relationship. Several formalized feedback systems also exist for assessing client progress in therapy. Lappan et al. (2018) provide a description and review of several of these formalized feedback systems. For example, you could administer the Outcome Rating Scale and the Session Rating Scale each session to monitor how therapy is going (Campbell & Hemsley, 2009; Miller et al., 2003). The Outcome Rating Scale is a four-item scale that is administered at the beginning of each session to assess how each client is doing in four areas: (a) individually, (b) relationally, (c) socially, and (d) overall. By graphing these scores over time, the therapist can evaluate if the couple is progressing. The Session Rating Scale is also a four-item scale, but it is administered at the end of the session to evaluate the quality of the therapeutic alliance.

When Therapy Is Not Progressing

If the clients are not making adequate progress, then you may need to consider a number of possibilities. The following questions can help you figure out why therapy is stuck. When considering each of the questions, be aware that more than one factor can be contributing to a lack of effectiveness in therapy.

First, is some important information about the couple missing? By using the assessment approach in this book, this is less likely to happen. However, there is also the possibility that a secret or critical piece of information (e.g., an affair) was withheld during an individual interview if you followed a no secrets policy.

Second, do you feel like an adequate therapeutic relationship has been established with both partners? Problems in the therapeutic alliance can result in resistance and therapy being less effective (Karam & Blow, 2020). As noted, the Session Rating Scale is one possible means for evaluating the therapeutic relationship on an ongoing basis.

Third, have you addressed any potential issues around commitment to the relationship? Although some ambivalence about a distressed relationship is common and to be expected, strong ambivalence can also undermine an individual's investment in making the necessary changes to improve the relationship. If one or both partners are seriously questioning whether to continue the relationship, then an approach like discernment counseling might be indicated (Doherty et al., 2015).

Fourth, are there any self of the therapist issues that may be contributing to therapy being stuck (Patterson et al., 2018)? Seeking consultation or supervision can help identify if this is an issue and how to manage it. In some instances, a referral to another therapist may need to be considered.

Fifth, have you given enough attention to identifying and altering the couple's vicious cycle? Chapter 4 discussed the importance of identifying the cycle. Losing focus on the cycle can sometimes lead to therapy becoming stuck, especially if you are using models where identifying the cycle is not strongly emphasized.

Sixth, is each person willing to look at their contribution to the relationship issues? Couples commonly come in with a blame-frame, essentially focusing on how their partner is responsible for the problems in the relationship. Movement in therapy can be a challenge if couples maintain this blame-frame rather than focusing on their own contribution to the relationship problems. Helping couples transition from a blame-frame to taking responsibility for their own contributions can help get therapy unstuck. For example, identifying cycles can help the couple recognize that each partner contributes in some manner to the problems in the relationship, even if it is unintentional.

Finally, should a different treatment model or approach be considered? Sometimes you may need to reconceptualize the case and take a different approach. Again, seeking consultation or supervision is recommended to explore this possibility.

Readiness for Termination

Another important part of assessing progress in therapy is to determine when the couple is ready for termination. One way to do this is to ask the couple directly about their readiness to end therapy. You can ask the couple if they feel like their goals have been accomplished, or if they are satisfied with the improvements in the relationship.

There are two potential problems that can arise when evaluating a couple's readiness for termination. First, some couples may be reluctant to stop therapy even if they believe that satisfactory progress has been made. They may have fears that stopping therapy will result in the couple sliding back into old patterns. Therefore, you may need to assess if a couple's reluctance to stop therapy is due to concerns about inadequate progress being made, or if it is attributed to anxiety about ending therapy. For example, I might ask a couple, "How will you know when you are ready to stop coming to therapy?" This will often illuminate if further changes need to be worked upon, or if it is just the couple's anxiety. If the latter, then a variety of interventions (e.g., offering reassurance, normalizing their anxiety, spacing out sessions) can help build the couple's confidence that they can resolve future issues on their own.

Second, some couples may perceive that they are ready for termination, but you believe the couple could benefit from doing more work. In these situations, the couple's autonomy and right to make a decision as to when to terminate therapy should be respected. However, the therapist will ideally do their best to prepare the couple for future challenges, including considering when it might be appropriate to return to therapy. In these circumstances, I will frequently ask clients, "How will you know if you need to return to therapy?" This can sometimes set the stage for the couple to reenter therapy if unanticipated challenges emerge.

Conclusion

One of the challenges in couple therapy is how to use all the information gained through assessment to develop an effective treatment approach. This chapter offers some guidance on how to do this. The chapter begins by examining the pros and cons of using an existing model or integrative approach therapy. If the therapist chooses to work from primarily one model, the chapter explores possible factors to weigh in choosing the model. Giving the couple feedback on their relationship and outlining treatment goals is another important element that is discussed.

This chapter also emphasizes that assessment does not end with the presentation of treatment goals, but it must be done throughout therapy. The therapist must continually evaluate whether the couple is making adequate progress, including when termination of therapy should be considered. In the event therapy is not progressing, the chapter offers some diagnostic questions that the therapist can reflect upon to assess why therapy might be stuck.

REFERENCES

Althof, S. E. (2014). Treatment of premature ejaculation: Psychotherapy, pharmacology, and combined therapy. In Y. M. Binik & K. S. K. Hall (Eds.), *Principles and practice of sex therapy* (5th ed., pp. 112–137). Guilford Press.

American Psychiatric Association (2013). *Diagnostic and statistical manual of mental disorders: DSM-5* (5th ed.). American Psychiatric Association.

Aron, A., Norman, C. C., Aron, E. N., McKenna, C., & Heyman, R. E. (2000). Couples' shared participation in novel and arousing activities and experienced relationship quality. *Journal of Personality and Social Psychology, 78,* 273–284. https://doi.org/10.1037//0022-3514.78.2.273

Balderrama-Durbin, C. M., Snyder, D. K., Heyman, R. E., & Haynes, S. N. (2020). Systematic and culturally sensitive assessment of couple distress. In K. S. Wampler & A. J. Blow (Eds.), *Handbook of systemic family therapy: Volume 3* (pp. 27–48). Wiley. https://doi.org/10.1002/9781119438519

Baucom, D. H., Epstein, N. B., Kirby, J. S., & LaTaillade, J. J. (2015). Cognitive-behavioral couple therapy. In A. S. Gurman, J. L. Lebow, & D. K. Snyder (Eds.), *Clinical handbook of couple therapy* (5th ed., pp. 23–60). Guilford Press.

Beck, A. T., Steer, R. A., & Brown, G. K. (1996). *Manual for the Beck depression inventory-II.* Pearson.

Bergeron, S., Rosen, N. O., Pukall, C. F., & Corsini-Munt (2020). Genital pain in women and men. In K. S. K. Hall & Y. M. Binik (Eds.), *Principles and practice of sex therapy* (6th ed., pp. 180–201). Guilford Press.

Bhugun, D. (2017). Intercultural parenting in Australia: Managing cultural differences. *The Family Journal, 25,* 187–195. https://doi.org/10.1177/1066480711399723

Birchler, G. R., Doumas, D. M., & Fals-Stewart, W. S. (1999). The seven Cs: A behavioral systems framework for evaluating marital distress. *The Family Journal, 7,* 253–264.

Blount, A. J., & Young, M. E. (2015). Counseling multiple-heritage couples. *Journal of Multicultural Counseling and Development, 43,* 137–152. https://doi.org/10.1002/j.2161-1912.2015.00070.x

Bograd, M., & Mederos, F. (1999). Battering and couples therapy: Universal screening and selection of treatment modality. *Journal of Marital and Family Therapy, 25,* 291–312.

Bradford, K. (2010). Screening couples for intimate partner violence. *Journal of Family Psychotherapy, 21,* 76–82. https://doi.org/10.1080/08975351003618650

Brimhall, A. S. (2020). Therapy with remarried and stepfamilies. In K. S. Wampler & A. J. Blow (Eds.), *Handbook of systemic family therapy: Volume 3* (pp. 317–341). Wiley. https://doi.org/10.1002/9781119438519

Brotto, L. A., & Velten, J. (2020). Sexual interest/arousal disorder in women. In K. S. K. Hall & Y. M. Binik (Eds.), *Principles and practice of sex therapy* (6th ed., pp. 13–40). Guilford Press.

Brunsma, D. L., & Porow, M. (2017). Multiracial families: Issues for couples and children. In S. Kelly (Ed.), *Diversity in couple and family therapy: Ethnicities, sexuality, and socioeconomics* (pp. 289–308). Praeger.

Buehler, S. (2017). *What every mental health professional needs to know about sex.* Springer.

Busby, D. M., Crane, D. R., Larson, J. H., & Christensen, C. (1995). A revision of the Dyadic Adjustment Scale for use with distressed and nondistressed couples: Construction hierarchy and multidimensional scales. *Journal of Marital and Family Therapy, 21,* 289–308.

Bustamante, R. M., Nelson, J. A., Henriksen, R. C., & Monakes, S. (2011). Intercultural couples: Coping with culture-related stressors. *The Family Journal, 19,* 154–164. https://doi.org/10.1177/1066480711399723

Campbell, A., & Hemsley, A. (2009). Outcome rating scale and session rating scale in psychological practice: Clinical utility of ultra-brief measures. *Clinical Psychologist, 13*(1), 1–9. https://doi.org/10.1080/13284200802676391

Chapman, G. D. (2010). *The 5 love languages: The secret to love that lasts.* Northfield Publishing.

Christensen, A., Dimidjian, S., & Martell, C. R. (2015). Integrative behavioral couple therapy. In A. S. Gurman, J. L. Lebow, & D. K. Snyder (Eds.), *Clinical handbook of couple therapy* (5th ed., pp. 61–94). Guilford Press.

Crippen, C., & Brew, L. (2007). Intercultural parenting and the transcultural family: A literature review. *The Family Journal, 15,* 107–115. https://doi.org/10.1177/1066480706297783

Davis, S. D., Lebow, J. L., & Sprenkle, D. H. (2012). Common factors of change in couple therapy. *Behavior Therapy, 43,* 36–48. https://doi.org/10.1016/j.beth.2011.01.009

Doherty, W. J., & Harris, S. M. (2017). *Helping couples on the brink of divorce: Discernment counseling for troubled relationships.* American Psychological Association. https://doi.org/10.1037/0000029-000

Doherty, W. J., Harris, S. M., & Wilde, J. L. (2015). Discernment counseling for "mixed-agenda" couples. *Journal of Marital and Family Therapy, 42,* 246–255. https://doi.org/10.1111/jmft.12132

Dürr, E. (2009). Lack of "responsive" sexual desire in women: Implications for clinical practice. *Sexual and Relationship Therapy, 24,* 292–306. https://doi.org/10.1080/14681990903271228

Edwards, J. N., Johnson, D. R., & Booth, A. (1987). Coming apart: A prognostic instrument of marital breakup. *Family Relations, 36,* 168–170.

Fetvadjiev, V. H., & van de Vijver, F. J. R. (2015). Measures of personality across cultures. In G. J. Boyle, D. H. Saklofske, & G. Matthews (Eds.), *Measures of personality and social psychological constructs* (pp. 752–776). Academic Press.

Fruzzetti, A. E., & Payne, P. (2015). Couple therapy and borderline personality disorder. In A. S. Gurman, J. L. Lebow, & D. K. Snyder (Eds.), *Clinical handbook of couple therapy* (5th ed., pp. 606–634). Guilford Press.

Funk, J. L., & Rogge, R. D. (2007). Testing the ruler with item response theory: Increasing precision of measurement for relationship satisfaction with the Couple Satisfaction Index. *Journal of Family Psychology, 21,* 572–583. https://doi.org/10.1037/0893-3200.21.4.572

Goldberg, L. R. (1993). The structure of phenotypic personality traits. *American Psychologist, 48*(1), 26–34. https://doi.org/10.1037/0003-066X.48.1.26

Gottman, J. M. (1999). *The marriage clinic: A scientifically-based marital therapy.* W. W. Norton & Company.

Gottman, J. M., & Gottman, J. S. (2015). Gottman couple therapy. In A. S. Gurman, J. L. Lebow, & D. K. Snyder (Eds.), *Clinical handbook of couple therapy* (5th ed., pp. 129–157). Guilford Press.

Gottman, J. M., & Silver, N. (1999). *The seven principles for making marriage work*. Three Rivers Press.

Gottman, J. S., & Gottman, J. M. (2015). *10 principles for doing effective couples therapy*. W. W. Norton & Company.

Green, R.-J., & Mitchell, V. (2015). Gay, lesbian, and bisexual issues in couple therapy. In A. S. Gurman, J. L. Lebow, & D. K. Snyder (Eds.), *Clinical handbook of couple therapy* (5th ed., pp. 489–511). Guilford Press.

Greene, K., & Bogo, M. (2002). The different faces of intimate violence: Implications for assessment and treatment. *Journal of Marital and Family Therapy, 28*, 455–466.

Hiebert, W. J., Gillespie, J. P., & Stahmann, R. F. (1993). *Dynamic assessment in couple therapy*. Lexington Books.

John, O. P., Naumann, L. P., & Soto, C. J. (2008). Paradigm shift to the integrative Big Five trait taxonomy: History, measurement, and conceptual issues. In O. P. John, R. W. Robbins, & A. P. Pervin (Eds.), *Handbook of personality: Theory and research* (3rd ed., pp. 114–158). Guilford Press.

Johnson, S. M. (2004). *The practice of emotionally focused couple therapy: Creating connection* (2nd ed.). Routledge.

Johnson, S. M. (2015). Emotionally focused couple therapy. In A. S. Gurman, J. L. Lebow, & D. K. Snyder (Eds.), *Clinical handbook of couple therapy* (5th ed., pp. 87–108). Guilford Press.

Kalogeropoulus, D., & Larouche, J. (2020). An integrative biopsychosocial approach to the conceptualization and treatment of erectile disorder. In K. S. K. Hall & Y. M. Binik (Eds.), *Principles and practice of sex therapy* (6th ed., pp. 89–111). Guilford Press.

Karam, E. A., & Blow, A. J. (2020). Common factors underlying systemic family therapy. In K. S. Wampler, R. B. Miller, & R. B. Seedall (Eds.), *Handbook of systemic family therapy: Volume 1* (pp. 147–169). Wiley. https://doi.org/10.1002/9781119438519

Karpel, M. A. (1994). *Evaluating couples: A handbook for practitioners*. W. W. Norton & Company.

Keirsey, D. (1998). *Please understand me II: Temperament character intelligence*. Prometheus Nemesis Book Company.

Kellner, J. (2009). Gender perspective in cross-cultural couples. *Clinical Social Work Journal, 37*, 224–229. https://doi.org/10.1007/s10615-009-0214-4

Kelly, S., Wesley, K. C., Maynigo, T. P., Omar, Y., Clark, S. M., & Humphrey, S. C. (2019). Principle-based integrative therapy with couples: Theory and a case example. *Family Process, 58*, 532–549. https://doi.org/10.1111/famp.12442

Kessler, R. C., Adler, L., Ames, M., Demler, O., Faraone, S., Hiripi, E., Howes, M. J., Jin, R., Scnik, K., Spenser, T., Ustun, T. B., & Walters, E. E. (2005). The World Health Organization adult ADHD self-report scale (ASRS): A short screening scale for use in the general population. *Psychological Medicine, 35*, 245–256. https://doi.org/10.1017/S0033291704002892

Killian, K. D. (2001). Reconstituting racial histories and identities: The narratives of interracial couples. *Journal of Marital and Family Therapy, 27*, 27–42.

Killian, K. D. (2012). Resisting and complying with homogamy: Interracial couples' narrative about partner difference. *Counselling Psychology Quarterly, 25*, 125–135. https://doi.org/10.1080/09515070.2012.680692

Knudson-Martin, C. (2013). Why power matters: Creating a foundation of mutual support in couple relationships. *Family Process, 52*, 5–18. https://doi.org/10.1111/famp.12011

Knudson-Martin, C., & Huenergardt, D. (2010). A socio-emotional approach to couple therapy: Linking social context and couple interaction. *Family Process, 49*, 369–384. https://doi.org/10.1111/j.1545-5300.2010.01328.x

Lappan, S., Shamoon, Z., & Blow, A. (2018). The importance of adoption of formal client feedback in therapy: A narrative review. *Journal of Family Therapy, 40*, 466–488. https://doi.org/10.1111/1467-6427.12183

LeBlanc, A. J., Frost, D. M., & Wight, R. G. (2015). Minority stress and stress proliferation among same-sex and other marginalized couples. *Journal of Marriage and Family, 77*, 40–59. https://doi.org/10.1111/jomf.12160

Lebow, J. L. (2019). Current issues in the practice of integrative couple and family therapy. *Family Process, 58*, 610–628. https://doi.org/10.1111/famp.12473

Leslie, L. A., & Young, J. L. (2015). Interracial couples in therapy: Common themes and issues. *Journal of Social Issues, 71*, 788–803. https://doi.org/10.1111/josi.12149

MacIntosh, H. B., Vaillancourt-Morel, M.-P., & Bergeron, S. (2020). Sex and couple therapy with survivors of childhood sexual trauma. In K. S.

K. Hall & Y. M. Binik (Eds.), *Principles and practice of sex therapy* (6th ed., pp. 371–394). Guilford Press.

Malouff, J. M., Mundy, S. A., Galea, T. R., & Bothma, V. N. (2015). Preliminary findings supporting a new model of how couples maintain excitement in romantic relationships. *American Journal of Family Therapy, 43*, 227–237. https://doi.org/10.1080/01926187.2015.1034634

Maltz, W., & Maltz, L. (2010). *The porn trap: The essential guide to overcoming problems caused by pornography*. HarperCollins.

Markman, H. J., Stanley, S. M., & Blumberg, S. L. (2010). *Fighting for your marriage: A deluxe revised edition of the classic best seller for enhancing marriage and preventing divorce* (3rd ed.). Jossey-Bass.

Maynigo, T. P. (2017). Intercultural couples and families. In S. Kelly (Ed.), *Diversity in couple and family therapy: Ethnicities, sexuality, and socioeconomics* (pp. 309–336). Praeger.

McCarthy, B., & McCarthy, E. (2014). *Rekindling desire* (2nd ed.). Routledge.

McCrae, R. R., & Oliver, J. P. (1992). An introduction to the five-factor model and its applications. *Journal of Personality, 60*, 175–215. https://doi.org/10.1111/j.1467-6494.1992.tb00970.x

McGoldrick, M., Gerson, R., & Petry, S. (2020). *Genograms: Assessment and treatment* (4th ed.). W. W. Norton & Company.

Michaels, M. L. (2011). Remarital issues in couple therapy. In J. L. Wetchler (Ed.), *Handbook of clinical issues in couple therapy* (2nd ed., pp. 189–204). Routledge.

Miller, S. D., Duncan, B. L., Brown, J., Sparks, J. A., & Claud, D. A. (2003). The Outcome Rating Scale: A preliminary study of the reliability, validity, and feasibility of a brief visual analog measure. *Journal of Brief Therapy, 2*, 91–100.

Mintz, L. B., & Guitelman, J. (2020). Orgasm problems in women. In K. S. K. Hall & Y. M. Binik (Eds.), *Principles and practice of sex therapy* (6th ed., pp. 109–133). Guilford Press.

Papernow, P. L. (2015). Therapy with couples in stepfamilies. In A. S. Gurman, J. L. Lebow, & D. K. Snyder (Eds.), *Clinical handbook of couple therapy* (5th ed., pp. 467–488). Guilford Press.

Patterson, J., Williams, L., Edwards, T., Chamow, L., & Grauf-Grounds, C. (2018). *Essential skills in family therapy: From the first interview to termination* (3rd ed.). Guilford Press.

Perelman, M. A. (2020). Delayed ejaculation. In K. S. K. Hall & Y. M. Binik (Eds.), *Principles and practice of sex therapy* (6th ed., pp. 156–179). Guilford Press.

Radloff, L. S. (1977). The CES-D Scale: A self-report depression scale for research in the general population. *Applied Psychological Measurement, 1,* 385–401.

Roddy, M. K., Nowlan, K. M., Doss, B. D., & Christensen, A. (2016). Integrative behavioral couple therapy: Theoretical background, empirical research, and dissemination. *Family Process, 55,* 408–422. https://doi.org/10.1111/famp.12223

Seshadri, G., & Knudson-Martin (2013). How couples manage interracial and intercultural differences: Implications for clinical practice. *Journal of Marital and Family Therapy, 39,* 43–58. https://doi.org/10.1111/j.1752-0606.2011.00262.x

Shreffler, K. M., Gallus, K. L., Peterson, B., & Greil, A. L. (2020). Couples and infertility. In K. S. Wampler & A. J. Blow (Eds.), *Handbook of systemic family therapy: Volume 3* (pp. 385–406). Wiley. https://doi.org/10.1002/9781119438519

Silva, L. C., Campbell, K., & Wright, D. W. (2012). Intercultural relationships: Entry, adjustment, and cultural negotiations. *Journal of Comparative Family Studies, 43,* 857–870.

Singh, R., Killian, K. D., Bhugun, D., & Tseng, S. T. (2020). Clinical work with intercultural couples. In K. S. Wampler & A. J. Blow (Eds.), *Handbook of systemic family therapy: Volume 3* (pp. 155–183). Wiley. https://doi.org/10.1002/9781119438519

Snyder, D. K. (1997). *Manual for the marital satisfaction inventory – revised.* Western Psychological Services.

Snyder, D. K., & Balderrama-Durbin, C. M. (2012). Integrative approaches to couple therapy: Implications for clinical practice and research. *Behavior Therapy, 43,* 13–24. https://doi.org/10.1016/j.beth.2011.03.004

Snyder, D. K., & Balderrama-Durbin, C. M. (2020). Current status and challenges in systemic family therapy with couples. In K. S. Wampler & A. J. Blow (Eds.), *Handbook of systemic family therapy: Volume 3* (pp. 3–25). Wiley. https://doi.org/10.1002/9781119438519

Spanier, G. B. (1976). Measuring dyadic adjustment: New scales for assessing the quality of marriage and similar dyads. *Journal of Marriage and the Family, 38,* 15–28.

Spitzer, R., Kroenke, K., & Williams, J. (1999). Validation and utility of a self-report version of PRIME-MD: The PHQ Primary Care Study. *Journal of the American Medical Association, 282*, 1737–1744.

Stanley, S. M., Rhoades, G. K., & Markman, H. J. (2006). Sliding versus deciding: Inertia and the premarital cohabitation effect. *Family Relations, 55*, 499–509.

Stith, S. M., Spenser, C. M., & Mittal, M. (2020). Couple violence: In-depth assessment and systemic interventions. In K. S. Wampler & A. J. Blow (Eds.), *Handbook of systemic family therapy: Volume 3* (pp. 99–121). Wiley. https://doi.org/10.1002/9781119438519

Straus, M. A. (1979). Measuring intrafamily conflict and violence: The Conflict Tactics Scale. *Journal of Marriage and Family, 41*, 75–88.

Straus, M. A., Hamby, S. L., Boney-McCoy, S., & Sugarmen, D. B. (1996). The Revised Conflict Tactics Scale (CTS2): Development and preliminary psychometric data. *Journal of Family Issues, 17*, 283–316. https://doi.org/10.1177/019251396017003001

Tannen, D. (2007). *You just don't understand: Women and men in conversation.* HarperCollins.

ter Kuile, M. M., & Reissing, E. D. (2020). Lifelong inability to experience intercourse (vaginismus). In K. S. K. Hall & Y. M. Binik (Eds.), *Principles and practice of sex therapy* (6th ed., pp. 202–223). Guilford Press.

Tili, T. R., & Barker, G. G. (2015). Communication in intercultural marriage: Managing cultural differences and conflicts. *Southern Communication Journal, 80*, 189–210. https://doi.org/10.1080/1041794X.2015.1023826

Tonelli, L. A., Pregulman, M., & Markman, H. J. (2016). The Prevention and Relationship Education Program (PREP) for individuals and couples. In J. J. Ponzetti, Jr. (Ed.), *Evidence-based approaches to relationship and marriage education* (pp. 180–196). Routledge.

Weiner Davis, M. (2003). *The sex-starved marriage: Boosting your marriage libido.* Simon & Schuster.

Weiss, R., & Cerrato, M. (1980). The marital status inventory: Development of a measure of dissolution potential. *American Journal of Family Therapy, 8*, 80–85. https://doi.org/10.1080/01926188008250358

White, M., & Epston, D. (1990). *Narrative means to therapeutic ends.* W. W. Norton & Company.

Whiting, J. B., & Crane, D. R. (2003). Distress and divorce: Establishing cut-off scores for the Marital Status Inventory. *Contemporary Family Therapy, 25*, 195–205.

Wiebe, S. A., & Johnson, S. M. (2016). A review of the research in emotionally focused therapy for couples. *Family Process*, *55*, 390–407. https://doi.org/10.1111/famp.12229

Williams, L. M., Edwards, T. M., Patterson, J., & Chamow, L. (2011). *Essential assessment skills for couple and family therapists*. Guilford Press.

Williams, L. M., & Lawler, M. G. (2000). The challenges and rewards of being an interchurch couple. *Journal of Psychology and Christianity*, *19*, 205–217.

Williams, L. M., & Tappan, T. (1995). The utility of the Myers-Briggs perspective in couple counseling: A clinical framework. *American Journal of Family Therapy*, *23*, 367–371.

INDEX

5 *Love Languages* (Chapman) 87–90, 92; acts of service 88–89; gifts 88; physical touch 89; quality time 88; psychoeducation on 162; words of affirmation 88

7 Cs: example of feedback using **165–166**; overview 1–6; treatment plan using 165–168; *see also* caring; children; commitment; communication; conflict resolution skills; contract; culture

10 *Principles for Doing Effective Couples Therapy* (Gottman and Gottman) 4

12 Step groups 117

16 Personality Factor Questionnaire 134

acceptance 5, 52, 56, 164; intercultural couple's struggle with 59

acceptance from others: culture and 69–72

acceptance of responsibility 128

accumulating trust *see* trust

acknowledgement of hurt 128

acts of service 88

ADHD: distraction during sex and 102; emotional dysregulation and 47; undiagnosed 16, 23, 141, 142, 147

Adult ADHD Self-Report Scale (ASRS v1.1) Symptom Checklist 142

affairs (marital infidelity) 81, 82, 128, 129–130; *see also* infidelity

affection, physical 113–114

agreeableness 135, 138

alcohol: abuse of 46; couples discouraged from talking while under the influence of 26, 49; sexual functioning impaired by 103; as subject of couple's conflict 61, 143; underreporting consumption of 19

American culture and society 60, 95

anger 37–38, 93; sex and 107, 109–110

answering why 129

atonement 129–130

anxiety 38, 166; chronic pain and 145; financial 53; neuroticism and 135; performance 101, 103–104, 107, 111, 118; sexual topics and 100, 169; sexual desire and 102; therapy, anxiety around 171–172

apology 128

argument, arguing 43–45, 145; bipolar disorder as source of 149; escalation 49; compulsive gambling as subject of 143; perpetual problems, PREP approach to 52; Speaker Listener Technique applied to 49; "weekly business meetings" (PREP) approach 51

Art and Science of Love 162

asking questions *see* questions

assessing progress during therapy *see* treatment plan for couples

assimilation 66–67

atonement 129–130

Beck Depression Inventory II 23, 142

betrayal 81; infidelity as act of 121, 129; secrecy and 116

Big Five Inventory (BFI) 136

Big Five personality traits 134–136, 137–138

Big Five Questionnaire (BFQ) 136

bipolar disorder 47, 142, 145, 147–149

Birchler, Gary 2

Blow, A. 54, 170

blueprint: couple's assessment 7, 161; family 61; relationship 123; tradition gender role 68

"blueprint war" 123

Bogo, M. 48

Bograd, M. 48

borderline personality disorder 46–47, 149

boredom 97, 114

Bringing Baby Home 162

cardiovascular disease 100, 102, 111, 148

caring and caring behaviors 5, 11–12, 86–99; assessing **98**; bidding for emotional connection 92–94; conflict and 87; different forms of 87–90; enhancing 50; offering emotional support 15; mutually rewarding activities 94–97; offering support 90–92; ritual 97; showing 84; uncaring behavior 33, 54, 55; see also 5 *Love Languages* (Chapman); sex and sexual relationship

CES-D 23

Chapman, G. 88

character 6, 11, 133–151; attacking
43; concerns regarding
13; emotional sensitivities
139–141; mental and physical
illness 141–150; personality
134–139; strengths, assessing
150–151
character features, assessing 12,
151–152
child abuse 15–16, 36, 48–49,
140; physical 104; sexual 106
childcare 68–69, 95, 110, 154
children 6, 153–158; assessing
couples who are also parents
153–156, **158–159**; conflict over
62, 64, 124–125; couples with
50, 84, 87, 95, 144; couples
that do not want 166; couples
where only one partner wants
124–125; custody of 80;
discipline of 156–158; as major
transition 14, 136; stepfamilies
156–158
Christenson, A. 11, 38, 52, 138,
139, 168, 169
clinical observation 20–22
closeness 33; bid for 34;
desire for more 53; differing
expectations of 123; lack of
107; sex as means of 108–109
coexisting couples 64
cohabitation 80
commitment 5, 75–84;
courtship and 11; dating and
cohabitation 13; dedication
and constraints 80–81;
factors impacting 77–81; fear
of 81; how to assess 76–77;
inventory of **84–85**; protective
factors for 82–84; sex and 12;
teamwork and 83
commitment dilemmas 81–82
commitment issues 77–80
communication 4, 25–41;
intimacy and 35–39; model for
understanding 25–35
communication sample
10–11, 21
compromise 52, 131; goal of 125;
possibility of 124; suitable 127
conflict: emotional dysregulation
during 46–47; flooding 44–46;
Four Horsemen (criticism,
defensiveness, contempt,
stonewalling) of 43–44, 46,
56; intimate partner violence
47–49; poorly handled 42–46;
protective factors in managing
49–51; types of problems
that can create 51–53; vicious
cycles and 53–55; see also
criticism; defensiveness;
contempt; escalation;
household chores; housework;
money; perpetual problems;
pornography; resolvable
problems; stonewalling
conflict resolution 42–56; PREP
ground rules 56; time-outs
45–46, 56
conflict resolution skills 5, 49
Conflict Tactics Scale 23; Revised
Conflict Tactics Scale 23
conscientiousness 134, 135

contempt 43, 45, 54, 56
contract *see* couple's contract
Couple Satisfaction Index 22
couple's contract 6, 120–132;
    accepting responsibility
    128; accumulating trust 130;
    acknowledging hurt 128;
    answering why 129; apology
    128; assessment of **131**;
    atonement 129–130; breach,
    dealing with 127; negotiating
    different expectations 123–126;
    renegotiating 126–127;
    unstated expectations 120,
    121–122
couple therapy: assessment
    instruments 21–23; clinical
    questions 19; how to begin
    6; five session model 6–19;
    observations 20–21; tools for
    assessment 19–20
courtship 11–13, 78, 83
Crane, D.R. 22
criticism 8, 43, 56
culture 5, 58–72; acceptance
    from others and 69–72;
    communication and 29;
    sociocultural context in
    the assessment of couples
    67–69, **74**
cultural differences between
    partners 59–63; managing
    63–67

dating: activities during 96;
    couple's patterns established
    while 63, 65; ritual of 95;
    sliding into marriage from
    79; unplanned pregnancy
    while 78
DBT *see* dialectical behavior
    therapy
DEEP analysis 139
defensiveness 35, 43, 56; cultural
    beliefs and 65
depression 23, 54;
    antidepressants 103, 109,
    111, 146; assessment
    instruments for 142; bipolar
    147; dismissiveness of 93;
    irritability and 145, 147; low
    sexual desire and 102–103,
    109, 111, 146; men suffering
    from 144–145; neuroticism
    and 135; physical reasons for
    143; pornography use to cope
    with 116; unipolar 143
desire for a family and children
    124, 154, 158
desire for sex *see* sexual desire
diabetes 102, 111, 119, 146
dialectical behavior therapy
    (DBT) 47, 163, 164
different expectations 121,
    123–126
different values *see* values
disciplinary role of parents
    156–158
dismissiveness 93–94
divorce 9; consideration of
    76–77; cohabitation more
    likely to end in 80; costs of
    splitting 79; likelihood of
    22; predictors of 43, 93; risk

factor for 94; seeds of 11; threatening 45

drinking see alcohol

Driver, Janice 93

drugs and drug use 46, 50; addiction 141; sexual functioning impacted by 103

Dyadic Adjustment Scale 22, 76, 169

dyspareunia 101, 112, 113

EFT see emotionally focused therapy (EFT)

emotional closeness/connection 53; bids for 92–94, 98; lack of 61; sex and 108, 109, 110, 113

emotional dysregulation 21, 163–164; conflict and 46–47; see also stonewalling

emotional expressiveness, lack of 60

emotionally focused therapy (EFT) 3, 4, 161; primary emotions 38; see also Socio-Emotional Relationship Therapy (SERT)

emotional harm 49

emotional intimacy: lack of 107; sex and 113

emotion-out-of-control 93

emotional sensitivities 52, 133, 139–141, 151

emotional support 5, 149 see also gift of advice; gift of understanding

emotional vulnerability see vulnerability (emotional)

emotional withdrawal 144–145, 167; see also depression

emotion–coaching 93–04

emotion-dismissing 93–94, 164

empathetic conjecture 162

empathy 39, 92, 94

Enneagram 134

erectile difficulties and dysfunction 101–103, 105, 111–112, 115, 146

escalation 35, 43, 44, 47; de-escalation 46; see also Speaker Listener Technique

Essential Assessment Skills for Couples and Family Therapists (Williams) 2

expectations 6, 130–131; contradictory 125; gender 62; importance of stating 127; realistic 104–105; unrealistic 69; unstated 121–122; see also couple's contract

external processor 26–28

extraversion 135–139

Eysenck Personality Inventory 134

family connections 60–61

family therapy 2–4; see also treatment plan for couples

fatigue 108, 142–143, 145

feedback for couples see treatment plan for couples

female sexual disorders see sexual disorders

filters 32–34

financial stress 144; *see also* money

Five Factor Personality Inventory (FFPI) 136

flooding 44–46

FOCCUS marital inventory 121

Four Horsemen (criticism, defensiveness, contempt, stonewalling) *see* conflict; contempt; criticism; defensiveness; stonewalling

Fruzzetti, A. E. 46, 47, 163,

gambling problem 143–144, 147

gender 31, 33, 57, 58; internalized messages regarding 59

gender differences 30, 90

gender issues and parenting 155

gender roles 62, 68–69

gender socialization 40, 55, 68, 93

gift of advice 91, 98

gift of understanding 90, 98

gifts: Christmas 157; love language of 88

Gottman approach 49, 92–94, 126, 139, 161–164

Gottman, John 3, 4, 42, 43–46, 49–51, 52, 92–94, 114, 126, 139, 162–163

Greene, K. 48

HEXACO Personality Inventory 134

Hiebert, W. 123

hormones 102

housework 54, 68–69, 77, 110, 126

Huenergardt, D. 67

hypothyroidism 102

IBCT *see* integrative behavioral couple therapy (IBCT)

IBCT approach 163

infertility 154–155

infidelity 6, 82, 121, 127–130; *see also* betrayal

inhibitions *see* sexual inhibitions

integrative approach 4, 160–163

integrative behavioral couple therapy (IBCT) 4, 38, 55, 139, 160–162

intermittent explosive disorder 47

internal processor *see* external processor

interracial couples *see* race and racial privilege

intercultural couples 5, 59–60, 62, 69; assessment questions for **72–73**

intimacy 36, 37, 39, 113

intimate partner violence (IPV) 9, 17, 21, 23, 47–49, 56

intimate relationships: challenges of 1; communication necessary for 4, 25; conflict as part of 42, 55; couple's contract for 120; dating as prelude to 95; distribution of power in 59; family history in relationship to 16; love as cornerstone of 5;

low self-esteem and 140; low
sexual desire in 104; mental
illness and 144; mutual
support as necessary in 90;
romantic relationships as
synonymous with 36; sex and
108; vulnerability and 67
intimate terrorism 48
introversion *see* extraversion
irritability 50, 143, 145, 150

jealousy 140, 156
Johnson, S. 138, 161

Karam, E. A. 54 170
Keirsey Temperament Sorter 137
Knudson-Martin, C. 64, 67

language abilities 60
Lappan, S. 169
Lebow, J. 161, 163,
love languages 97, 113; *see 5 Love
Languages* (Chapman)
Loving Couples Loving
Children 162
loyalty 61, 70; issues for
children 157

macroagression 70
male sexual disorders *see*
masturbation; premature
ejaculation; sexual disorder
Maltz, L. 116
Maltz, W. 116
marginalization 70, 71, 156
marriage 1–3, 7; attempting to
heal 129; children and 157;

cohabitation prior to 80;
cultural challenges to 66,
70–71; female subservience
during 77; lack of sex during
107, 109–110; mental health
impacts on 142, 148–149; poor
health and 81, 145; sex and
pregnancy prior to 13, 44, 61,
79; vows 82
masturbation 100–102, 112;
delayed ejaculation caused
by 111; using pornography
during 116
McCarthy, B. 99, 105, 106, 113
McCarthy, E. 99, 105, 106, 113
Mederos, F. 48
medications 103, 109, 111, 144
mental health disorders 47,
102–103; ruling out 109
mental illness 6; challenges
posed to couple by 133,
141–150; emotional
dysregulation and 46; history
of 17; impact on relationship
143–146; managing 146–150;
undiagnosed 142; vicious cycle
143–144
meta-emotion mismatch 94
meta-emotion style 93–94, 164
microagression 70, 71, 72
minimization strategy 63–64
minority couples 71
minority stress 5, 71
money: conflict and concerns
over 79, 95, 120, 158; different
orientations toward 51–53;
pooling 79; pornography,

spent on 115; power
differential due to 69, 157–158
Myers-Briggs 134, 136–138

negative emotions 43–44, 56,
    93, 135
negative impacts: affair 128;
    conflict and children 156;
    depression 142; mental or
    physical illness 141, 143, 145,
    150, 151; messages carrying 32;
    pornography 114; sexual abuse
    140; shame 104; trauma 106;
    violence 48
negative interactional patterns
    14, 21, 143, 155
negative judgements 36, 39
negative reactions 28, 30,
    32–33, 54
negative sentiment override 50
negatives impacting sex life 99,
    104–105, 114–116
NEO Personality Inventory,
    Revised (NEO PI-R) 136
neuroticism 135

observation see clinical
    observation
open-ended questions see
    questions
openness 135
orgasm 101–104, 108, 111;
    diabetes interfering with
    146; difficulty achieving 115;
    primary anorgasmia 112;
    sexual inhibitions and 106
Outcome Rating Scale 169–170

Papernow, P. 156
parenting and cultural values 62;
    see also children
performance anxiety see anxiety
perpetual problems in couple's
    relationship 14, 51–54, 56;
    personality differences as
    basis for 133–134, 138
perpetuating negative or vicious
    cycles 38, 47, 53–54, 144
personality features see Big Five;
    Myers-Briggs
Peyroine's disease 112
PHQ-9 23, 142
physical abuse 46
physical illness 6, 133, 141–151
physical touch 89
Please Understand Me II
    (Keirsey) 137
pleasurable activities 96; failure
    to prioritize 138; reduction
    in 145; self-care 148; wrongly
    prioritizing 134
pornography use 100, 105,
    114–117
power dynamics 5, 59, 60, 62,
    68–69, 123; changes in 144;
    cultural factors influencing
    5, 13, 62, 67, 73; imbalanced
    125; see also pursue-withdraw
    dynamic
pregnancy: delaying 154; inability
    to achieve 124; unplanned
    13–14, 78–79; unwanted 14;
    see also birth control; infertility
premarital inventory 122, 131
premarital sex 61

premature ejaculation 103, 110–111
PREP *see* Prevention and Relationship Enhancement Program (PREP)
PREPARE premarital inventory 121
Prevention and Relationship Enhancement Program (PREP) 4, 34, 162, 163; positive strategies for couples provided by 49–50, 52, 56, 82–83
primary anorgasmia 112
primary emotions 38
primary model of therapy 161–163
psychoeducation 162–164
PTSD 16, 23, 47, 102
pursue-withdraw dynamic 44, 53, 167

questions, open-ended or closed-ended 19–20, 94

race and racial privilege 71, 72; interracial couples 69–72, 165
RELATE marital inventory 122
relationship blueprints 123
relationship history 10, 11, 78, 83
relationship issues and sex 107
religious difference 58, 62, 66
resentment: from children toward stepparents 157; examples of 27, 34, 68; caregiving and chores as source of 77, 148–149; family obligations as source of 61; major illness in spouse as source of 127; personality differences as source of 134; pornography as source of 115; power imbalance as source of 125; religious values as source of 66; sexual demands as source of 110
resolvable problems 51–52, 56
respectful engagement 64–66
rituals 97

same-sex couples 69, 70, 71
self-care, assessment of 147–149
self-disclosure 38
self-esteem 82, 128, 129, 130, 139–140
self-soothing 46
sensate focus 104, 169
sensuality and physical affection 113–114
separating person from illness 149–150
serenity prayer 52
Seshadri, G. 64
sex and sexual relationship 99–117; assessment questions for **117–119**; ability to communicate about 114; general assessment guidelines for therapists 100–102; pornography 114–117; protective factors 113–114

sex education 112
sexual abuse 140; *see also* child abuse
sexual addiction 117
sexual behaviors 114
sexual desire 101–104, 107–110, 112–116; depression and 146; past trauma and 167
sexual disorder 101–102; common causes of 102–106; female sexual disorder 112–113; male sexual disorder 111–112; specific considerations regarding 107–111
sexual fetishes 106, 111
sexual inhibitions 106
sexual intercourse, inability to tolerate 146
sexual intimacy 20, 89, 98; emotional connection and 113; mental and physical health, impact on 145–146
sexual pleasure 104
sexual preferences and orientation 106–107
shame 104, 122, 140
Shreffler, K. 155
Smart Recovery 117
social support 149
sociocultural assessment of couples **74**
Socio-Emotional Relationship Therapy (SERT) 67–68
Speaker Listener Technique 34, 46, 49

Stanley, S. 80
stating needs 150
stepchildren 153
stepparent 156–158
stonewalling 43–44, 56
Structured Initial Interview 11, 23
substance use 103
suicide 17, 146

Tannen, D. 33, 90–91
Taylor Johnson Temperament Analysis 134
testosterone 102
trauma 106; sexual 167
treatment plan for couples 160–172; assessment during therapy 168–170; developing 160–165; therapy not progressing 170–171; providing feedback using 7 Cs 165–168; termination of therapy 171–172
trust: accumulating 130; building 8; difficulty and issues with 15, 36, 140; rebuilding 129; violation of 36

unstated expectations *see* expectations

vaginismus 112–113
validation 35, 39, 90; invalidation 38, 47, 91, 130
values 8, 51, 82; authoritarian-military 157;

different 61, 115; parenting and 62; religious 116; shared 65
vicious cycles 14, 46, 53–55; caring/not caring caught in 87; couple's power struggle 68; mental/physical illness caught in 143–144; sexual desire caught in 109–110, 115–116; *see also* perpetuating negative or vicious cycles
vulnerability (emotional) 21, 36–40, 52, 55; difficulty with 67–68; reluctance to share 75

Whiting, J. B. 22
words of affirmation 88, 90

Lightning Source UK Ltd.
Milton Keynes UK
UKHW021957120223
416799UK00032B/418